This Is Your Brain on Shamrocks

T0171596

Mike Farragher

authorHOUSE®

AuthorHouse™
1663 Liberty Drive
Bloomington, IN 47403
www.authorhouse.com
Phone: 1-800-839-8640

First published by AuthorHouse 1/21/2011

ISBN: 978-1-4567-2684-3 (e)
ISBN: 978-1-4567-2683-6 (sc)

Library of Congress Control Number: 2011900163

Printed in the United States of America

Foreword by Niall O'Dowd

Mike Farragher is not the kind of guy you'd want at your wedding, funeral, or bachelor party.

But you'd want to read his book.

He's too observant for your own good and he will catch that funny moment when you least expect it.

It makes great reading *unless* you're the subject.

The bride drops her drawers? Mike will catch it. The coffin falls out of the hearse? Mike will be there, gimlet eye seeing all. Then he'll toss off some devastating riff on your wedding/funeral etc. and you will be shamed for life.

That's it.

The nice part is, he does it to himself, too.

He did a piece not long ago for the *Irish Voice* on his devastating attraction to women that his wife must have loved, knowing no one of the fair sex would have come within a country mile of him after reading it.

Then there was the recent piece about the Irish and penis size—but I digress—luckily for Mike.

He has the gift, you see. This New Jersey son of Erin has the insight of the Druids, the perspective of a high king and the pen of a major poet. He knows the Irish like his own skin (which he has also written about), knows our foibles, our fantasies, our "fecked" up view of creation.

If he had been St. Patrick he'd have had the locals laughing and converting in hours. "Did you hear the one about the High King and the horse's ass?" he'd say, then go off on some funny riff.

Mike is your brain on shamrocks, an Irish kid from New Jersey who bleeds green, knows the scene, and is funny and mean.

Well, rarely mean. Among his other hats, Mike is a tremendous writer about Irish music in all its facets.

If there's an up-and-coming Irish band in Poughkeepsie, Mike will sniff them out. Not only that, he'll promote the hell out of them until they get the break they deserve.

He has been the expert on the Irish music scene for over a decade now. But lately his "narrowback" roots have been calling, and Mike has been writing.

This book is a respectful look at the glorious traditions of the Irish in America. *Not.*

He's a rebel, a poet and a trailblazer.

So enjoy this extraordinary book. And if you see Mike on the guest list at one of your special events—bar him.

—Niall O'Dowd
Founder, Irish Voice *newspaper*
Irishcentral.com
September 2010

Contents

This Is Your Brain On Shamrocks.

It's not just a catchy title of a book that I pray will lift me from relative obscurity into a lifestyle cushier than the one I am living now. It's also a metaphor for the influence an Irish upbringing has on American children.

The previous generations coined a term for people like me: we're called *narrowbacks,* and rest assured, gentle reader, that is not a term of endearment.

We come from a hearty stock of people who developed broad backs from the hard labor that comes with the territory of a rural Irish farm.

As the story goes, our ancestry came to America and put their kids through school so that they wouldn't have to endure the hard life of their parents. Their dream of making a better life for their kids soon backfires once the kids are catapulted into the kind of social class that allows them to hire people to care for their children, clean their houses, mow their lawns… in short, perform the same handyman jobs their parents did when they first arrived to America. The once proud parents would look in disgust at the soft hands and lack of muscular definition that the "good life" brings. "Feckin' narrowback wouldn't know an honest day's work if it bit 'im on the arse!"

This is just one of the dynamics of an Irish-American upbringing that I dissected in my bimonthly "Narrowback's Corner" column in the *Irish Voice.* If I am a shamrock, then my roots are tangled in a compost of debilitating Catholic guilt, repressed sexuality from years of nuns shepherding impure thoughts with corporal punishment, and a shadow of doubt that the other shoe is about to drop whenever you find yourself at a peak in your life. To be uncomfortable when things are good is to be an Irish narrowback.

I thought I was the only one who had a mother who would get me out of bed on a Sunday morning by screeching, "I'm sure the Lord Jesus Christ didn't want to get up the day he died for your sins," but I was wrong. I got e-mails, Facebook posts, and letters to the editor by the dozens from Irish-Americans in my age bracket telling me that I was writing about their lives as well. I was unprepared for the reaction and deeply grateful for the many people who encouraged me along the way.

One person who was not in my corner as these articles hit the newsstands was my mother. At first, she constructed this Angela McCourt nightmare scenario in her mind. She raised a writer son who would be doing a "hatchet job" on her in the same way Frank did on *Angela's Ashes*.

Nothing could be further from the truth and in time, I think my mother eventually came around to see these essays for what they really were: an attempt to share the humorous stories of an unremarkable Irish upbringing and honor the family by keeping those stories alive for the next generation of our family.

Sure, my mother and father were the dumbest people I knew during my teenage years but as I grow older with kids of my own, they look smarter with each passing year. They are sensible, selfless, hardworking people who strived to deliver the best they could to their sons by managing whatever life threw at them, and I dedicate this book to them.

I would also like to acknowledge friends and family who encouraged me along the way: Dennis Duffy and his crazy sisters Deb, Siobhan, Mimi, and Denise, Armando Llanes, Margaret Duffy, Sue Gallagher, Theresa McNamara, Theresa Cleary McKnight, Georgiana Cleary, Kevin McGrath, Billy Steets, and Larry Kirwan.

A special acknowledgment must be given to Cormac MacConnell, my colleague and friend at the *Irish Voice*. His "West's Awake" column was the weekly benchmark for me throughout this writing process; he set a high bar of storytelling excellence that I tried to emulate or exceed, with results that were marvelous and mixed depending on the essay. Thanks to Debbie McGoldrick and Niall O'Dowd, who gladly gave up real estate in *The Irish Voice* and IrishCentral.com to carry out this literary experiment.

Thanks to Phil Duffy for his loyal friendship, legal counsel, and making me look good in the publicity photos. I cannot possibly repay the debt of gratitude to Brian Blatz for his literary surgery. As editors go, Brian is the best coach a writer could have and the best friend a guy has the right to hope for. Thanks to Kevin Adkins for a brilliant cover design!

My wife Barbara is an inspiring, bold partner in my life and I love her for putting up with me. I found the memories of my own childhood jogged by my current parenting situation and I thank my beautiful daughters Annie and Maura for their inspiration and love. I am so very lucky to have this kind of family unit.

Let's be clear on one thing: everything in this book is factual but not everything in it is true. I went on memory, which is always a dangerous thing. In any case, you're not going to see me atoning for literary sins on Oprah's couch the way James Frey did during the *Million Little Pieces* backlash.

Though Frey has sold many more books than I have, I know something he may not: Never let the truth get in the way of a good story.

The Travel Agents for Guilt Trips

Living in sin, with sin, by sin, for sin, every hour, every day, year in, year out. Waking up with sin in the morning, seeing the curtains drawn on sin, bathing it, dressing it, clipping diamonds to it, feeding it, showing it 'round, giving it a good time, putting it to sleep at night.

I'm not sure if the writer Evelyn Waugh was an Irish Catholic, but when he wrote those lines in *Brideshead Revisited, The Sacred and Profane Memories of Captain Charles Ryder* in 1945, he described perfectly the oppressive chokehold that sin and the guilt of an Irish mother have on our soul.

You remember the definition of "near occasions of sin" from the *Baltimore Catechism*: "all the persons, places, and things that may easily lead us into sin."

Not very specific, is it? That was all part of the plan. To make sure we all color inside the lines, the Catholic education system labeled everything as sinful and to avoid sinning, we were taught to stay clear of just about everything that was pleasurable.

Being Catholic means sliding out of the birth canal as a sinner, which is why as babies, we were swaddled in white clothes and taken to the church within days of birth so that the stain of Original Sin could be removed from our souls in the sacrament of Baptism. You wouldn't want your kid to live for a few days, only to die and go to Hell like a dead bulb that never blooms into a tulip, would you?

We were taught that the human condition is like the Gulf of Mexico waters: God made this pristine ecosystem for us to pollute with black poison that spewed from a pipeline of our wrong choices and sinful ways. I could almost sign up for that, but how do you explain a baby being blemished with the ink of sin from Day One? It is one of the many contradictions in our faith that defies logic.

If Catholic school was our foundation of guilt, our mothers were the travel agents for the guilt trip. I remember many a Sunday morning when a Saturday night bender made it near impossible to get up for church.

"I'm sure Jesus didn't want to get up the day he died for your sins," my mom would say.

"I didn't ask him to do that for me," I'd reply in defense, but the damage was done.

With those words, she would start a grease fire of guilt in my bed that consumed me until I could no longer stand the heat of the covers.

"I remember getting the '10 stitches speech' growing up," recalled one friend on the barstool next to mine as we compared notes on our Irish mothers. "She'd look forlorn and say, '10 stitches. 'Twas 10 stitches they used to sew me up after I had you and if I knew you were going to (insert bad deed here), I would have never went through the pain of birthing you!' She was unreal."

I think that one had my mom beat and I pray she is not reading this. She doesn't need any more ammunition!

Through marriage to a Jewish woman, I have discovered that mothers in that faith do a number on their kids as well. I remember my father-in-law winning the Physician of the Year award for his cutting-edge cancer care at one of the large hospitals in New Jersey. We all attended the awards ceremony.

"You must be so proud of your son that he won this," gushed one of the nurses to his mother.

His mother rolled her eyes.

"He should win the award for man who calls his mother the least," she said with a grunt.

Sure, I can tell myself all I want that I am 44 years old and I have finally broken free of my mother's influence as I raise my own family.

But I know I am an Irishman, which means that my mother will be in the sidecar commenting on every pit stop on my route. When I flip through *The New York Times* on my luxuriant deck on any given Sunday, a little voice that sounds remarkably similar to hers says, "When you miss Mass, you damn not only your own soul, but the souls of my granddaughters who don't get to go based on your bad example." When I try to cut down on the portions at dinner and empty food into the garbage disposal, that voice gently reminds me that there are starving "mission babies" in Africa who would kill to have what I am throwing out.

"Dude, there's medicine for that," my friend at the bar says, rubbing my shoulder as he shakes his head when I say this out loud.

Yeah, right. An Irish mother's guilt is etched in your soul. Kinda like sin, apparently.

Tattoo You

I want to get a tattoo. Two, actually. Both would adorn an ankle on each leg.

The first one would have some design incorporating the first letters of Annie, Maura, and Barbara (daughters and wife, respectively) meshed into a big "F" that represents my last name.

The second would depict the CelticLounge.com logo. CelticLounge was a website that I developed with Larry Kirwan of Black 47. Long before Facebook caught fire, the two of us saw a need to connect Irish artists with fans online. Though it was a money loser that ultimately folded, I was intensely proud of what we created and I bought myself an education on how e-commerce works. By tattooing that logo on my ankle, I could look down and be reminded that even the chances you take that ultimately fail can enrich your life in the long run because it pushes you outside your comfort zone.

Or some bullshit like that. You catch my drift.

The urge to "get ink" is particularly strong this week, as I am vacationing in Wildwood, New Jersey, and I feel as though we are the only family walking the boardwalk that *isn't* tattooed. Tattoo parlors sit beside games of chance and cotton candy vendors here; if you hanker to win a stuffed frog or tattoo Kermit above your nipple, it can be accommodated here.

I have been noodling this idea with my wife for some time, who is neither here nor there about it.

"You know what would be hot? Why don't you get one of those tribal tattoos around your bicep?" she suggests.

She is thinking about the depiction of blackened barbed wire that circles the bicep of our neighbor Carlos, a tanned and Portuguese George Clooney lookalike upon whose body everything looks good.

If I put that on my thin and pale arm, it would look like a French fry in bondage. Not exactly sexy.

Two things are stopping me from taking the inky plunge. First, there is the sour expression of my mother as she's surveying my new artwork. I've played out her speech in my mind a thousand times.

"Well, 'tis your life and your body," she might say in her Limerick accent. She might even throw in a shrug for good measure, pretending not to be bothered with the news.

"Of course, as I gave birth to you, after nine of the most agonizing pushes any human being would have to endure, I never imagined at the time that ye'd defile yourself with graffiti 44 years later. Had I known that, sure I don't think I would have bothered to push and wail at all.

"But, sure, what would I know? I'm just an old lady with old-fashioned virtues. I don't understand kids today or how ye parent nowadays. I certainly don't understand what would possess an eejit of 44 years of age that has gone this long without doing something that stupid to break his perfect track record now.

"You never saw your father get a tattoo, so I know you didn't get this crazy idea from the example we set. And of course, the example ye'll set for your daughters will just be great, luv, wouldn't it? They'll probably want to run right out and get one based on your inspiration. Anyway, I'm really glad ye said something to me now because it gives me time to get to church and say a novena that the good Lord knocks some sense into you before ye do something stupid. But again, 'tis your body. Ye do with it what ye want."

That conversation never actually happened, but that's what living under a cloud of Irish Catholic guilt at all times looks, sounds, and feels like. You have heard so many sermons like it that when a new ethical dilemma is put in front of you, like getting a tattoo, you have enough material from soliloquies in your past that you can cut and paste an entirely new one together to fit any occasion.

My mother, if she had the opportunity to say all that, has a point. I certainly don't want my kids to get a tattoo any time soon and when they reach legal age and leave for college, I don't want them thinking that they can ink themselves because Dad did it. Therein lies the second reason that stops me from getting inked.

My daughters are preteens now, and I have this recurring nightmare of them in a tattoo parlor dressed in their high school graduation caps and gowns. They are bent over the chair, legs spread and gown lifted to their shoulders, preparing for the installation of what is known as a "tramp stamp" at the base of their spine. In the dream I am a mere spirit in the corner and unable to be seen or heard as the whirring of a needle comes perilously close to their pale flesh.

When my own kids are faced with a decision to tattoo or not to tattoo, I pray that common sense will prevail. If not, I'll settle for a heavy-handed sermon of guilt, one possibly delivered in a Limerick accent, to save the day.

Crime and Punishment

I was hot under the collar when I sent that text message to my daughter and for those of you who are tech-savvy, you know that sending a note in capital letters denotes shouting in cyberspace. I meant business, yesirree!

While she was at a sleepover with her friends, I caught her sending text messages taunting her little sister and I wanted to avoid the seeds of cyber bullying from taking root with some swift and decisive action.

My iPhone buzzed a few seconds later.

"Sorry Dad. Didn't mean to," read the incoming text.

"Ride the bike home and think of the right punishment on the way," came my reply. I knew my mother would blink back tears of pride for allowing the errant child to stew in her own juices as she pedaled home. It was a lesson I learned from mom, and to say I learned from the best is an understatement.

Technology has transformed what modern scolding and punishment looks like nowadays and that is sad. Something gets lost in translation with this methodology compared to how my mother did it. She didn't use a digital screen to communicate and she didn't exercise her fingers on the rotary phone to call me home. Rather, she used the expansiveness of a white canvas known as the pillowcase to paint her rage in the most vibrant colors imaginable.

I was a bit careless in covering my tracks back then, and the evidence my bloodhound of a mother effortlessly dug up while cleaning in my room was substantial: hidden progress reports in which I forged her name, albums snuck into the house that had the Parental Advisory sticker on them, a cache of skin magazines, and liquor bottles that fell out of my college laundry bag were just some of the things she found. Each one of those items was placed on the pillow for me to address with her at the time of my choosing.

Think about the messages that gesture sent.

1. I found this.

2. You're going to have to brush this aside before your head hits the pillow tonight.

3. If you know what's good for you, you won't brush this aside.

4. I'm ready to rumble when you are.

My mouth would run dry and my palms would sweat, my breathing reduced to little gasps that would asphyxiate a rabbit. The stress and terror was the beginning of the punishment itself, and that was the point. That long walk out of my room and down the stairs was hell, making my calves tremble at the prospect of facing the music. There would be yelling to be sure. She might even throw in a "I didn't raise you in my womb for nine months for you to carry on like this" for good measure, but the punishment was fair, balanced, and rarely severe. It was the suspense of not knowing what evil lurked in the kitchen that was the most excruciating part of it all.

I used to think this tactic was unique to my mother, but unscientific research conducted on barstools throughout Manhattan recently confirmed that many Irish mothers out there did the same thing.

"Oh, dude, I hated that," groused a computer programmer friend of mine. "Even now, my eyes dart over to the pillow every time I walk into a bedroom, thirty some-odd years later. She's psyched me out with that shit, and she's still in my head."

That statement caused us to toast and shake our heads in agreement.

"I remember when my mother found my girlie magazines under the mattress once," recalled my friend John. "She put the stack of them on the pillow and then placed a King James Bible on top of that."

That got a round of belly laughs at the bar. It was a veritable guilt sundae, served up as only an Irish mother could, with the word of the Lord transforming into the maraschino cherry atop smoldering rage as dark and hot as molten fudge.

"My mother was this concierge of guilt, when I think about it," he continued. "She would give me a Bible to reflect on what I did and on the inside cover, she would tape a schedule of Confessions that she tore from the church bulletin."

My mom never did that. But the Confession schedule, along with that of all the Masses, was taped on the inside of the kitchen cabinet and as she poured me a shot of shame from the cupboard, she would have all the pertinent information necessary to repent and cleanse my wretched soul.

I am blessed with wonderful children who almost never give me trouble, but I won't short-sheet them with a text message next time I have to mete out punishment. I'll use the pillow method; that'll learn 'em!

Parenting Is for the Birds!

They walked in and if you've ever been a parent, you'd know that look anywhere.

My Limerick-born cousin and his American wife were negotiating their way through the door, her belly round and low with their next child and his shoulders saddled with all sorts of baby gear. They were completely wrung out, scarcely able to call after the 2-year-old that had darted out beneath their legs in hot pursuit of the hissing fat cat in the corner.

"It won't be long now," chirped my wife as she greeted the couple. "How are you feeling?"

"We haven't slept in weeks," was the breathy and exasperated reply. "We can't get the wee one to stay in her room—she's been sleeping in with us every night."

"Getting a kid out of your bed is like burning a tick off your skin," I said, the shaking head and dopey grimace dripping with judgment. My wife rewarded that ill-timed tidbit with a dirty look, in a night that was full of them.

My wife is a giving and nurturing soul; that said, good luck getting into our bed if you don't belong there. Sick children with high fevers and dogs with cold noses are banished from what she calls "my only quiet place away from all this madness" and even when my snoring gets too loud, I am unceremoniously ejected from the mattress.

They say all boys marry their mother, and in this instance, the saying rings true. Within our small apartment in Jersey City, my parents played traditional roles: he worked double shifts so that we could one day buy a house in the suburbs while she took care of the kids and kept the house. This meant she was stuck inside a cramped apartment 24/7 with two rambunctious male toddlers, so it was perfectly understandable that she would need some solace in the house. My mother might have watched me like a hawk as a kid but when it came to keeping me from wandering out bed in the middle of the night, she relied on a sparrow to stand watch when she was getting ready for some much needed shuteye.

It was a simple plaster statue, no more than seven inches tall, with an emerald- green head and a brick-red body. For some reason, the sight of that fake sparrow terrified me in the years leading up to kindergarten and my mother used it to full advantage.

My room was off to the side of the kitchen and before she went to bed, the bird would be set atop the counter, right next to my door. If I stepped out in the middle of the night, I would come face to face with my cold-eyed nemesis.

I might be fuzzy on the details as to whether or not the bird had dark green tail feathers glued to the arse end of it, but I will never forget those eyes—two white brush strokes with a black line down the middle. Cold, unblinking windows of the stone soul within that only came to life in my nightmares, when the winged hellion would pin my shoulders to the mattress with her talons and frantically pluck out my veins and intestines like worms in the soft earth.

When I recounted this story of the plaster sparrow to my friends not long ago, the women in the group cackled in mock horror. "Oh, my God, that is the most delicious child abuse story that I've ever heard," squealed one of them. I found myself at that moment rushing to my mother's defense. Sure, there was frequent bedwetting and an irrational fear of flapping wings, but abuse? Come on! Looking back, it occurs to me that this little sparrow was worth its weight in gold and I applaud my mother for the ingenious way she kept the puppies from running the dog pound when we were small. After all, the notion of having kids sleep in the bed with their parents is—pardon the expression—for the birds!

The Blood Clot with Wheels

This is the week of graduation and your heart has to go out to the cap and gown crowd walking down the aisle of their commencement ceremony and into the worst job market of a generation.

I know one girl who's gonna be all right. I spotted her at the dealership when I was getting my 45,000-mile service done. Her head was bent and the fingers were flying around the small keyboard of her cell phone like a hummingbird on nectar, no doubt texting her friends about the new Hummer that dad was buying her for graduation. She mugged for dad briefly, fixing him with the daddy's-little-girl look that all dads know as the cheese ball salesperson placed a giant red bow on the dashboard of this yellow monstrosity.

It kinda reminded me of my college graduation, when my dad and mom gave me my first car—except there was no showroom, salesperson, or red bow involved in the transaction that I can recall.

Now that I think about it, there was a vague promise of a new car if I produced the same good grades as my cousin Diane, a pharmacy major who tossed her cookies at the remote possibility of getting a "B." Once I collided with booze and loose women, which happened 48 hours after the first semester began, the car escaped my grasp. I remember coming home that first December; my dad looked up from reading the report card and said, "There's good grades and then there's a complete waste of overtime pay. Guess what this is?"

I didn't live up to my end of the car bargain with my summa-cum-lucky GPA and after commencement, I got the keys to a car as well as my comeuppance.

The car in question was a 1982 Ford Escort with no color contrast whatsoever; the paint was red, which perfectly matched the cloth interior, steering wheel, console, controls, and the dashboard.

My dad had a white government car that the New Jersey Turnpike issued to him, so he bought the Escort as "the second car" that he took on the second and third jobs he sometimes worked when the ends were not quite meeting in the house. When he wasn't driving it, my mom took it to the diner where she waited tables, bringing the car back reeking of hash browns.

Since everything was red inside and out, I looked like I was driving a blood clot with wheels when I went to pick up a girl on a date. If that sight weren't enough, the smell inside the car would kill any chance for romance.

I got a summer job working at a germicide company, where I spent one summer filling containers that hung above urinals with a sickeningly sweet chemical that masked the smell of the crap that flushed down the drain. Spills into the carpet of the trunk were inevitable, making the back seat smell like an industrial-strength cotton-candy-scented urine cake.

As soon as I had gotten the keys, I drove to Kmart for a leopard-print elastic cloth cover for the steering wheel in an attempt to cover up the grime that was etched into the hard plastic. The dirt was hammered into the wheel by the gritty grip of my parents and in my hollow vanity, I covered up this reminder of my socioeconomic status the first chance I got. A fuzzy-dice air freshener hung limply on the rearview mirror, no match for the fermented germicide cooking in the trunk's carpet on a hot day.

No matter how I "tricked out" the Escort, it was still the powerful vehicle my parents used to drive a hard lesson into me. It was one thing to drink and drug my way through college, but real life was a bumpier road that might smooth itself out when you buckle down and apply yourself.

While some of my classmates "found themselves" during a European backpacking trip after graduation, I spent my first months out of school working as hard as I could to get out of the blood clot. I worked as a customer service rep during the day and a bartender at Bennigan's in the evening and when the dealership served up the keys to a used 1986 Volkswagen Golf that September, I felt an enormous sense of accomplishment.

My taste in cars and the ability to buy the finer things in life have steadily increased over the years, but I still think of the bumpy ride on that blood clot with wheels every time I sign a new lease on a luxury vehicle.

I can't help but feel bad for the poor college grad that drove that Hummer off the lot last weekend; a 1982 Ford Escort is a much better vehicle when you want to give your ambition a little acceleration in the fast lane.

Irish Wake

I was there to pay respects to Rose Fitzgerald, a dear friend and joyous lady who had just completed living 88 rich years. Though illness had ravaged her body and mind these last few months, my mother was at her bedside the day before she died and reported that Rose was in fine voice as the pair sang the old Irish songs. How lucky would we all be to enter into eternal life with those beloved melodies tucking us into our long slumber?

The church's Rosary Society clan was huddled around the casket and as I knelt to pay my respects, I could hear a few sniffles and sobs escaping the pursed lips below their sculpted cotton-candy hairstyles. I knew that as I stood, stiffened my back and greeted these old Irish matriarchs, they weren't standing this close to the coffin just to reflect on their own mortality. The critique had begun.

"Doesn't she look gorgeous?" said one softly. "Sure, the blue suit she picked out was a brilliant choice."

"Aye," another one replied, shaking her head in disbelief. "Yeh half expect her to sit up and do the jig! Fair play to her that she raised kids that knew enough to buy priest vestments in her honor."

Anyone with an Irish mother of a certain age knows that they become experts in the art of putting the best foot forward when someone eases on down the road to their eternal reward. As she advances in years, Mom has transformed into some Heidi Klum on the set of Project Rigor Mortis.

Case in point: this fit-as-a-fiddle woman led me into her bedroom during a family gathering not long ago; she closed the door for privacy and I was sure I was going to either hear juicy gossip or get lectured again for not attending church on Sunday. She flung open the closet and pointed to a garment bag.

"This is the outfit I want to be laid out in," she said matter-of-factly.

"Did you get some news that would lead you to believe you'll be wearing that anytime soon?" I asked nervously.

"No, yeh eejit! Ye've got to plan for these things, and I don't trust your brother with this detail. And don't mess this up or I'll haunt yeh!"

That's something my mother has been threatening me with a lot in recent years. When she inventoried the curio cabinet full of Hummel and Norman Rockwell ceramic figurines, she had walked me through what was to be left to me and what was being left to my brother.

"What the hell am I going to do with this?" I asked.

"Well, what are you going to do with it?"

"Sell it," I replied.

"You wouldn't!"

"I would. In fact, you'll barely be cold before every piece in here will be posted on eBay."

Mom leaned into me and grabbed my shirt.

"You do that and I'll haunt you!" she hissed through clenched teeth.

I had seen firsthand how this obsession with looking good in the coffin could get out of hand. I'll never forget the fiasco with the undertaker when my good friend John lost his battle with diabetes. His mother was a white-haired Irish battleaxe from Yonkers whom everyone called "The Widow Dunn." She peered into the coffin of her son with her thick eyeglasses, frowned, and bit her lip. Was this callused bird about to break down?

"Take him out and change his clothes," she replied flatly. "No son of mine is going to be laid out in a black suit when he's lying in a brown box."

"Excuse me?" asked the flustered undertaker.

"Any idiot knows black and brown don't match," was the response.

"Change his clothes or I'm wheeling him out the door and onto Route 9, taking him home, and doing it myself." In the thirty minutes before show time, they had exhumed the body from the wood box and dressed it in a blue pinstriped suit.

They say the difference between an Irish wedding and wake is one less drunk, and I just hope that everyone is nursing a wicked hangover after a long night of laughter before they lower my casket into the ground. When that time comes, I will instruct my daughters to bury me in my best Tommy Bahama camp shirt because I am sure where I am going will be on the hot side of warm to say the least.

My Family Has Gone to the Dogs

I was trying to keep my cool, the only sign of my irritation emitting from the thumbs that drummed the handle of the shopping cart.

My daughters were fighting in the aisles of Petco, trying to decide which collar would best fit around the neck of Sophie, our beloved Chihuahua-Pug mix. One was made of pink leather, adorned with faux jewels, and the other was a strip of pink nylon with multicolored peace signs stamped into the fabric.

"I don't like either of them," I replied when asked to place the tie-breaking vote. "Since I am the one that walks her most of the time, I would like to vote for something more masculine or dark to butch her up a bit."

The girls rolled their eyes and returned to their shopping while I left for the far less glamorous task of picking out a bag of dog food. As I navigated the cart through aisles stocked with designer sweaters, canine bottled water and doggie diapers, I was grateful that 3,000 miles of ocean water separated me from Uncle Paddy's farm in Tuam.

Don't get me wrong: Paddy loves children and would love to spend the afternoon catering to the every whim of his grand-nieces.

"By jaysis, a girlene that gorgeous would want a prettier collar than that," he would say, chuckling to himself as he winked at me.

Sadly, Uncle Paddy is among the last of a dying breed of gentleman country farmers on the west side of Ireland. At 80, he still does his farming chores in a pair of Wellington boots that miraculously match the suit pants and jacket he wears regardless of the weather. His rugged face is deeply lined, creased around the mouth to revel a long life of laughter, and his ruddy complexion amplifies his Paul Newman-blue eyes.

Let's just say that through those eyes, he looks at pets a bit differently from how we do over here. Animals in that neck of the woods aren't beloved family members that require fuss and pampering; rather, they exist to work the land alongside the farmer, nipping at the heels of a stray calf or killing the mice that have the misfortune of squeezing under the kitchen door.

As kids, I remember my father (Paddy's younger brother) recalling how they would choose the heartiest dog or cat from the litter and throw the rest of the animals in a burlap sack to be hurled into the river. I took my girls to Galway a few years ago, and they had taken a shine to one of the mutts that patrolled the farm. I remember when a neighbor's dog brushed up against my daughter. He was struggling a bit after eye surgery, his head contained in a cone the kept him from scratching at the stitches.

"What's his name?" one of my daughters asked Paddy. He bent down and met their gaze.

"By God, it's been so busy around here that we didn't get a chance to name him. Any ideas?"

They looked at the poor mutt with one shut eye and named him Winky. We all laughed.

"Winky it is," Paddy proclaimed. He suddenly turned his back on the girls and directed the next sentence at me.

"Winky here is a bit slow; I'm not sure the little fellah is going to work out for that neighbor."

I went back a year later and there was another collie mutt patrolling the barn in place of Winky, who was probably an hour into a long dirt nap under some dung heap by the time our family had cleared customs at Shannon Airport.

You might think Uncle Paddy is insensitive and barbaric, but nothing could be further from the truth. He is the favorite uncle in the family and there are two generations of children with our earliest memories of Ireland attached to the giddy thrill of riding the old horse Tom around the farm under his watchful eye.

This view of animals is not fostered out of callousness; anyone witnessing how Paddy reduces himself to a puddle of tears whenever the Yanks board their Aer Lingus flight home knows that this is a man who feels deeply.

The fact that my uncle wouldn't be caught dead watching *Animal Planet* is just something cultural, plain and simple. That doesn't make it right, mind you, but it does make you look long and hard at the ridiculous lengths to which we go for our pets on this side of the Atlantic. As with most things in life, a reality check somewhere in the middle is in order.

Paddy probably won't let an animal's love into his life at this advanced age, but maybe I will put my foot down and say no next time the receptionist at the Boarding Barn offers to videotape Sophie's stay at the kennel for $20 per day. I'll just pay my $10 for the vitamin-infused doggie drink, thank you very much.

So, knowing the pecking order of dogs in my ancestry, the introduction of an American veterinarian into our family provided an interesting wedding to say the least! When my brother was bent on one knee and asking for the hand of his girlfriend Laurie, he also had to ask for the paw of Mylo, her adorable white West Highland Terrier with the dreamy brown eyes.

It was about this time eight years ago that my parents' house was aflutter in guests from Canada and the auld sod that flew in for Brendan's big day. The morning of the wedding found the stress level to be at fever pitch and after announcing to my mother that he needed a house full of company on this day like he needed "another set of balls," Dad was all too happy to run an errand over to the bride's house for a relief from the bedlam.

He returned a short while later and I noticed him pacing at the foot of the stairs, the calloused hand smoothing his widow's peak of hair as he walked. Growing up in the house, I knew these gestures to be akin to the steam before the geyser erupts. He caught my eye and pointed in the direction of the half bath on the first floor, the only refuge in a house full of relatives running around with curlers in their hair.

Getting two burly Irishmen into that small space was no small feat and we found ourselves nose to nose.

"I just came from the mother of the bride's house and that feckin' dog is in a tuxedo! What do you know about this?"

"N-nothing," I stammered. "I bought all the tuxedos and I would have told you if I picked up one for the dog."

"Yeh think they have better sense than to bring that animal into the house of God?"

"Of course they have enough sense," I replied before breaking into our favorite Clancy Brothers tune:

All God's creatures have a place in the choir

Some sing low and some sing higher

Some sing out loud in the telephone wire

Some just clap their claws or paws or anything they got now.

At this point, Dad informed me that he needed a comedian right now like he needed "another set of balls" and stomped out of the washroom.

As soon as the service was over, Mylo hopped out of the limo and trotted by the newly married couple at the foot of the stairs to join the reception line like he belonged there, which of course he did. My father shook his head and let out a defeated groan as the photographer's camera whirred behind him.

"We'll be the laughingstocks if this makes it over to Galway," he whispered before putting on his best game face as my brother's newly minted in-laws fussed with the pooch a few feet away.

The happy couple is holding the leash together and beaming as they descend the church steps in the photo that was sent overseas with each thank-you note. My little cousins in Galway adored the picture, the novelty of it all delighting them to no end.

The picture said it all: a new family was standing proud on all eight legs for the whole world to see. The dog (mercifully) skipped the reception but not before he left a lasting paw print on our hearts.

Mylo is like the Rosa Parks of the animal kingdom, refusing to ride the back of the bus as he ushered in an animal-rights movement in our family. My father and mother now feel naked if they walk in my door without a chew toy for our Sophie and each "grand-dog" gets a stocking full of treats on Christmas.

Our family has gone to the dogs and in the words of Martha Stewart, that's a good thing.

The Meat of the Matter

On Father's Day, I plan on doing what I always do: hosting the old man for a steak on the grill cooked by a deeply appreciative son.

On the morning of his arrival, I will go to the town butcher and I get what's called a butter steak; it is a long, thin strip of heifer doused in a brown, gravy-like balsamic vinaigrette mixture that caramelizes around the meat and traps in the juices as it heats up.

"I don't know how you get it perfect every time, but you do," he usually says, shaking his head and savoring the first mouthful for a second longer than the others.

My secret? It's simple: I take the steak off the grill before every last drop of juice evaporates out of it. I'm not sure how it is in other Irish families, but in mine, we overcooked everything.

A typical Sunday pot roast dinner at the homestead involves a grey slab of dehydrated carcass that has congealed gravy dripping from it, garnished with potatoes and carrots boiled into Jell-o. We joke that mom's specialty dish is "black arsed buns," made from a sleeve of Pillsbury dough formed into disks that emerge from the oven enveloped in more smoke than a car crash. If I had a dime for every baking sheet that was thrown out because the black dough permanently spot-welded itself to the metal, I could hire a full-time sushi chef in the house.

Speaking of, don't even *think* about serving any *raw* fish wrapped in rice at one of my backyard barbecues this summer, lest you get a lecture on the dangers of putting uncooked food in your gob. "'Tis crawlin' with parasites, is what I read somewhere," one aunt might say, grimacing like she just downed a mouthful of buttermilk. "Och, sure, they eat the lining in your stomach once they hatch from eggs in that raw fish."

I remember well the first time I had a real pork chop; I was at a dinner party that my friends threw and I could only marvel at the delicious pink meat that clung to the Y-shaped bone. I didn't even know the color of a pork chop growing up; Mom would serve a tasteless piece of parchment in a thick coating of Shake 'n' Bake that was soggy on the bottom with what little grease was left in the animal after prolonged baking.

In her defense, she does make a killer soda bread and can usually turn out a good Thanksgiving turkey with a modicum of moistness. The culinary sins of overcooking meat come from my father, which is unbelievable when you consider that he was raised in a house which knows their meat like no other.

My grandmother Bridget (Lynch) Farragher was a no-nonsense woman, a thin ball of pipe-cleaner limbs bursting with energy.

Underneath thin strips of dyed brown hair severely pulled back into a bun were two blue eyes that didn't miss a trick, like a bird of prey scanning the countryside for three blind mice.

Once or twice a year, she would point a slender finger at one of the calves on the farm, which was separated from the rest. The animal would be fed only the finest grains and oats over the next few months, fattened with the best that the Galway soil would grow before the "creature" was sent over to Concannon's Butcher in town for storage.

She would greet the shopkeeper a few days later with a tight smile and order provisions for her husband and six kids from the calf stored in his freezer. Concannon's worst nightmare would come at him hard the next morning if there was an error.

"That was not my meat," she would say, those blue eyes pushing him into a corner. "I know what my meat tastes like and that wasn't it."

It sounds like an old wives' tale, but the people in Tuam know the difference between Outback steak and the sweet meat created from whole oats and barley. Even today, the 80-year-old son of Bridget, my father's brother, cannot be fooled when a strange piece of steak is put in front of him and he almost never goes to a restaurant because he hasn't formally met the cow that greets him on the plate.

It's a far cry from the scene at the grill at my house.

"What part of the cow does this butter steak come from?" Dad might ask, and once again, my blank expression will display what a hopeless narrowback I am.

For his Father's Day gift, however, I'll know exactly where the cow came from....Omaha Steaks!

Bridie's Coming

Those two words strike terror in the hearts of my parents.

My father had barely had time to replace the phone onto its hook after Bridie called to announce her visit last year before my mother vaulted onto the sofa, steadying herself on the arm of the couch as she tore down the curtains for dry cleaning. Dad scurried around her, shoving a drop cloth against the molding on the floor before removing the pictures on the wall.

"Make use of yourself, for God's sake: run to the Home Depot and get white paint!" he bellowed over his shoulder at me while steadying a stepstool.

A little background. Bridie is an impeccably dressed, ageless beauty from County Galway and despite whatever might be going on in her head, her face is always the picture of calm. She was the perfect foil for my Uncle John, a short Jack Russell terrier of a man with an endless supply of kinetic energy. She met John here in the States, even though they grew up only a few miles from one another in the Athenry area. They lived in the same Jersey City neighborhood as we did and John worked the New Jersey Turnpike with my dad for a number of years before moving back to Kilskeagh. Some of my fondest memories as a child were the big Sunday dinners at her house.

Their home was impossibly immaculate at all times, in spite of the fact that she had three kids under the age of ten running around. Clear plastic covers clung for dear life onto the cushions of the couch and you could manufacture microchips to your heart's content at the kitchen table because there wasn't a speck of dust visible in the air or on the surfaces. The house always smelled like chemical lemons, every inch of wood shined with Pledge before company arrived.

Every dish was (and still is) served out of the oven at the perfect temperature with nothing burned. The food stays hot throughout the whole meal and one begins to wonder after a while if there is uranium or some other radioactive substance is at play under each dish, keeping the food at ambient temperatures.

God inexplicably ended the vibrant marriage when He took my uncle a few days past his 60th birthday and the shock and sorrow is still raw throughout the family. Though she misses him deeply, I suspect she buries her grief in the nutrient-rich soil of her garden, where the stunning bouquets stand at attention on either side of the door in the event that the man of the house comes around to inspect them.

I tell you all this because the hot meals, clean house, and manicured garden have done a number on the Irish matriarchs' psyche in the family on this side of the Atlantic. Bridie has set an impossible standard by which my mother and aunts could never live up to and it drives them nuts.

"Would yeh clean up this mess!" If I had a dime for every time my mother screeched these words at her two small boys, we could have afforded a cleaning lady to tidy the place up a bit. "You don't see this kind of pigsty at Bridie's house, the Lord save us and guard us! Those kids help their mother and I am just wondering to myself what I ever did to God that He plagued me with such slobs!"

Mattresses flipped? Check. Smudges scrubbed from the walls that have just been freshly painted? Check. Lines from the vacuum's wheels neatly etched into the carpet? Check, check, check!. OK, we're ready for the visit!

It's one thing to tidy up a bit when company is coming, but do we really have to paint and remodel before the Aer Lingus wheels hit the tarmac at JFK? Why in God's name do we put ourselves through this stress? Is it a desire to portray the image to the visitors that we have it all together and live life in an impossibly clean way? Why are we so obsessed with looking good and why can't the family look past our Yank flaws and accept us for the imperfect people we are?

Though she walks in perfectly accessorized, a white glove is never part of the package. She looks you in the eye when she talks and is too busy responding graciously to your hospitality to make figure-eights with her finger in the dust on your mantle. After she goes home and we open our thank-you notes, there's never any mention of how clean everyone's house was. I consider that written proof that she is more focused on who is in the house than the house itself.

I shared a laugh with one of my wife's Scottish girlfriends last week; she is a teacher stressed out over the end of semester activities while juggling the remodeling of her home.

"Your house is a doll house; what do you possibly need to do in there?" say I.

"I've got visitors from Edinburgh coming next week," she gasped. "The pressure's killing me! My mother told me I'd better get my house in order so that 'the Yanks' don't look bad."

I chuckled at the ridiculousness of it all but stopped laughing when I opened my e-mail and got a note from Bridie's daughter, Debbie, who announced she was coming with her boys for a visit in a few weeks. The note was forwarded to me from my cousin Diane, who announced that she was putting an immediate stop to her search for a second home near me to spend the summer getting the house ready for Debbie's visit.

Armed with a rag in one hand and a can of Pledge in another, I logged off of e-mail and tore at the house in a lemon-fresh cloud.

Helicopter Parents

I just heard the phrase "helicopter parents" for the first time; it is apparently a name given to parents who hover around their children in an attempt to protect them from even the slightest pitfalls and disappointments in life.

"Heard about it? I live it!" That was the response of my sister-in-law, a director of one of the many divisions at New York University's admissions office. "When the rejection letter comes in the mail, some parents take it upon themselves to contest our decision and plead with us to reconsider because the kid is not accustomed to rejection. Can you imagine that?"

Actually, I can't. I'm not sure I ever actually saw a helicopter in my childhood and if I did, I can guarantee you that my mother and father were not at the controls.

I had what could best be described as plow parents; they were the ones who would steer the plow pulled out front by one of their kids and weren't afraid to pull out the whip if the plow was moving too slow or outside the lines.

If the nun sent me home with a bad grade or if I got detention, it was never the nun's fault. Dad would get out the belt and plow me into next week for upsetting the bride of Christ and he could not care less about my side of the story.

I was told by a staffer at my job's human resources department that helicopter parents even hover in the workplace! He has fielded more than one call from the parent of a recent college grad who felt that the kid's first boss was being unfair to their twenty-something tyke.

I do remember my mother calling one of my bosses once, but it was because she didn't feel as though I was working hard enough.

I had come home from college in the summer of 1986 with a report card that was on the wrong side of pitiful. While some of my wealthier friends were traveling through Europe or frolicking in the Caribbean in an attempt to rest up for another grueling semester, my mother saw to it that I stayed home and worked. I performed a series of warehouse and manufacturing jobs with a temp agency. For a few weeks, I trotted around pallets with a roll of shrink wrap in a sweaty cosmetics factory. After that, I wore a hair net and a white lab coat and stuffed powdered sugar into placebo caplets for a local pharmaceutical firm. When those shifts were done, I mowed lawns until it got so dark that I couldn't see the lines the mower made in the grass.

I would drag myself home, grimy with sweat and hobbled by aches and pains. I could see my parents' milky blue eyes dance with delight as I gripped the rail of the steps on my way up to the bathtub, where I would soak my pains away in a hot and salty bath.

I wanted to chase after them with the toilet plunger at the time, but I am now old enough to appreciate how a good old fashioned Irish plow can get you farther in life than a helicopter.

Book 2: Religion
No Hanky-Panky When He Is Around

There's nothing worse than seeing a grown man cry, so I cringed a bit as my buddy was reduced to a puddle of tears on the barstool next to mine. I could feel the guy's pain; he found his barely teenage daughter passed out in their basement the night before, the evidence of both sexual and alcoholic misadventure strewn across the floor around her. She was only a year or two older than my Annie, which made me swallow hard. Once again, this modern-day dilemma reminded me of what a genius my mother was.

There were no shenanigans like that going on in her house when we were teenagers and do you know why? Herself placed a Sacred Heart of Jesus painting in every room. Mind you, these were not depictions of Jesus' true to life portrait, with the almond complexion, dark eyes, and jet black hair of his Middle Eastern lineage. Rather, these were images the Irish are more comfortable with; saucer eyes of blue, a neatly trimmed goatee that blends into the body wave of luxuriant sandy blond curls framing the porcelain complexion without blemish. A luminous heart shines through His tunic while it sheds tears of blood, as do the hands, which are outstretched to show the wounds from the crucifixion.

The Lord might work in mysterious ways, but my mother doesn't. She instinctively knew that even if I were able to eject her from the house long enough to smuggle a girl in—assuming I could actually find a decent-looking girl despite my fat and pimply state—she left the house in His hands and that there was no escaping His gaze.

As my girlfriend and I wrestled our clothes off the one and only night I tried something in this environment, I couldn't help but catch a glimpse of those sad blue eyes. He wasn't *staring* at us, was He? Was He looking up to his Father in heaven or was He rolling his eyes at you, as if to say, "Dude, I hung on a cross in the middle of a desert for three hours to wipe away your sins and this is what you do with your second chance?" Was that a garbage truck rattling or a rumble of thunder and if those were storm clouds...was He going to fry my fat naked white ass with a bolt of lightning? Mom knew there was no way impure thoughts could fuel your libido with that going on in your head, and she was right.

You might wonder why I didn't just turn off the lights, but mom thought of that, too. Being the Rosary Society President meant that she had first pick over the latest merchandise in the annual religious-articles sale and over the years, she amassed an inventory of holy trinkets around the house that rivaled the largest kiosks on the road to Knock! The same image of Jesus on the wall was fashioned into a ceramic night light keeping watch in the hallway, the red bulb of a heart plugged into the wall emitting eerie scarlet rays that matched the hue of your sins. Of course, a door frame would look naked without a holy water dispenser nailed to it. Ceramic plates depicting each of the Stations of the Cross hung every few feet in the hallway.

Since my wife is Jewish, we have only one religious reference on the wall: a straw St. Bridget's cross over the front door. Irish folklore has it that this "keeps the fairies out," but my gay friends snort with laughter and point out its impotence. But now that the hormones rage in my 12-year-old, I'll be picking up an item or two at the in-house convenience store at the church.

Hell 2.0

I just came out of the mandatory Communion class that all parents must attend prior to their child's first sacrament of Reconciliation experience and I am in shock. The nun, an ebullient Irish cherub who long ago ditched the severe confines of the habit and veil long ago in favor of a Tara brooch and a sensible green pantsuit, stood in the musty cafetorium (the new word for the versatile room that houses the cafeteria and auditorium) and said something about the sacrament of Confession that robbed me of my breath.

"Sin is what happens when you know what you do is wrong but you do it anyway." Did I miss a Vatican III that applied white-out to the harsher passages on sin within the pages of the *Baltimore Catechism*? In my day, sin was painted as the poison to the soul that resulted in the "loss of heaven and the pains of hell" instead of the convenient momentary lapse of judgment as it is portrayed today. That wasn't the most shocking thing she said, however.

"Confession is a joyous time in a child's life," she proclaimed, the letters in her words affixing themselves to lines of sheet music as she sang them. "Many people dread the sacrament, and they shouldn't. For our God is a forgiving God, not a punishing one if the child is contrite. He only forgives."

Not a punishing God? *Really?* Surely, this nun didn't go to the Catechism class in the same convent as Sister Rita (the name has been changed to protect the ol' gal), the servant of God who taught my sex-education course at the turn of the Eighties in Jersey City. I remember well how my hormones were raging to break free of the confines of the desk at the time, yet I was terrified to move under the watchful eye of the woman we affectionately nicknamed "Fish Face."

This was an unsightly woman with thick bifocals and moles tucked in the scaly creases of her face. Her large lips were perpetually curled in a snarl; in the minds of an impressionable youngster, she bore more than a passing resemblance to the Creature of the Black Lagoon in a wimple. To mask the swamp rot in her gills, she would apply the allure of chemical flowers found in a Jean Naté bottle (no doubt given to her by parents courting her for mercy on their child).

In Sister Rita's world, sin was the furthest thing from a harmless lapse of judgment. Her delight as she described Hell was palpable; the way the Earth periodically parted to burp out the stench of burning flesh, the cold gurgling sludge of eternal suffering, and the loss of the Lord's light. How you got your ticket punched for a one-way trip to eternal damnation was the favorite part of her lecture.

"Violating your body with pleasures of the flesh before marriage is a mortal sin," she shrieked. "A mortal sin produces a macula that stains the soul and if it is not immediately repented in Confession, you will be eternally separated from God in Hell. If you die and a mortal sin is not confessed and repented for at the time of your death, it will result in damnation."

Everyone collectively swallowed hard as she said this. Despite her best efforts to suppress it, a satisfied smirk escaped her reptilian lips. With those words, she knew that you would never have a peaceful instant of carnal pleasure for the rest of your life.

To this day, she haunts my dreams. In a fantasy that has me locked in Nigella Lawson's passionate embrace with Janet Jackson waiting in the wings (hey, a guy can dream!), Sister Rita is propped up on the next pillow asking me to write "I will not pet the dolphin" on the chalkboard one hundred times.

I attended a personal-empowerment course recently and the facilitator defined that little voice in your head not as your conscience, as was taught in Catechism. Rather, he proposed that the voice was the thing that talked you out of being fully powerful and self expressed.

Welcome to my head. That little voice for me is Sister Rita, standing at the ready with a rosary bead dangling out of one dried-out claw while she holds the *Baltimore Cathecism* with the other. She stands with perfect posture, ready to extinguish all carnal pleasures the moment they catch fire.

My daughter will be receiving Communion this May without the blemish of a care on her face and a pure heart that loves her Maker, and I have a loving servant of the Lord stationed in the school at the end of Sesame Street to thank for that.

Ch-Ch-Changes

"This is the big change that signals you are growing from a child to an adult. It's a whole new experience, but it doesn't have to ruin your day."

Whoever wrote that didn't direct it at an Irish American father, for it is just as hard to write the words on this page as it was to read that sentence the first time I picked up the pamphlet titled "It's a Girl Thing." The school dropped it in my daughter's book bag as a parting gift at the end of the school year; it also served as warning to parents that *the video* was being viewed in health class by the fifth-grade girls this week.

There was no denying that my little girl was growing up. I could no longer trick myself into thinking that this was someone else's training bra I was throwing into the wash, assuming I had the stomach to touch it in the first place. The dark, brooding clouds that would form behind my Annie's pupils and change her mood at the drop of the hat was definitely a sign that the storm of puberty was coming.

So, I eyed the pamphlet on the kitchen countertop for a solid week before even chancing to open it. In a stroke of branding genius, I noticed that Kotex had prepared the brochure in an attempt to be well positioned when opportunity dropped, so to speak.

Like every man who needs to concentrate on an important document, I took the pamphlet into "the porcelain library." I began to get lightheaded when the words started rushing at me. *Vulva. Cervix. Endometrium. Ovulation!*

'Twas fortuitous that a toilet was underneath me, because by the time I hit the sentence that finished with the words "between a few teaspoons and a quarter cup of blood per cycle," I emptied the contents of my stomach into the bowl.

"Are you okay in there?" asked the 9-year-old younger sister from the other side of the door.

"I just got hold of a bad burrito; I'll be fine," I muttered weakly as I clawed at the sides of the toilet. Of course, I wasn't.

Why was I having this violent reaction? I have made a nice living selling diagnostic tests to detect the onset of disease states and I could probably pass the medical boards after sitting through countless physician conferences, so none of those words or concepts was foreign to me.

Was I having a hard time facing the fact that my kid was no longer a baby? I'm sure that was part of it. More likely, the vast majority of my discomfort probably stems from my learning about the birds and the bees from the Catholic school system. Despite conning myself into thinking I had evolved, I had to face the fact that my adult sexuality was a mere crouton floating atop a scalding soup of repression, Irish guilt, and shame.

I remember when I first heard about *the video*; at the time I was a few years older than my daughter is now. The nurse appeared at the classroom door one day and with one affirming nod to Sister Celine, the boys were shuttled into the hall as a television and VCR were wheeled into the room.

"The girls are watching a movie about changes in their bodies, and I want to talk to you about yours," said the nun.

Well, Sister, I'm glad you brought that up. We didn't have the benefit of Google in the Seventies and my body did not come with an owner's manual. I was praying that someone would explain why hair grew in some places and not others, how to tame certain body parts, and why I felt all fluttery when Miss Kemp walked by. Sister Celine liked to describe herself and the other nuns as "brides of Christ," but I was convinced that with Miss Kemp's clicky heels and tight-fitting fashions, the Man Upstairs would probably have the bartender walk past the nuns and place a drink in front of said math teacher on any given Saturday evening. I would sit through her class in agony as the hormones poured out of my body like maggots in hot garbage and I was hoping, above all else, that Sister Celine would give me tips on how to pull my grades up in Miss Kemp's class. .

"Many of you have noticed changes," she began. "Hair is growing on you and you may even begin to smell bad odors coming out of you. We would like for you to begin wearing deodorant under your arms from now on. Sometimes, the stench is unbearable in the classroom."

The old Polish nun began to pace now, her sensible shoes squeaking on the linoleum as she walked. Her upturned lip did little to hide her disgust and discomfort.

"Some of you may have urges or impure thoughts. These are sinful and could remove you from God when you die."

Period. End of story. Sister Celine had nothing for me. There would be some other references to touching yourself inappropriately in religious-education classes through the rest of grade school, but it wasn't until high school that Brother Bernardine gave it to us straight-up with no chaser.

He was a kind, lazy bear of a man from Louisiana, the slow drawl masking a quick wit and supreme intellect. We were in Latin class in this all-boy Catholic high school, and even Brother Bernardine would love to escape the rigors of verb dissection in the ancient tongue through an occasional side story. He asked us how the dating was going; since no girls were digging the Osmond-retaining-water look I was sporting at the time, I had nothing to contribute to the conversation. Of course, the towheaded swimming studs were all too eager to speak up, taking the opportunity to brag about their conquests to the rest of us. Brother Bernardine smiled and nodded knowingly; he had them just where he wanted them.

"You know what you're doing is a mortal sin against God, right, boy?" With his drawl, the word "boy" sounded like "boa." Like the snake of the same name, he was constricting the air out of his prey in front of our very eyes. "Having sex with someone you're not married to is gonna land you in hell. You also might be tempted to have your mind wander into dirty thoughts and then your hands will follow. You do know that's a mortal sin, too, right? I just wanna see y'all in heaven with me, that's all."

You could have heard a pin drop.

You might be wondering where my parents were during all of this?

41

The first time sex was mentioned, to my recollection, was not until college; I had begun regular activity in the dorm rooms with a fetching woman who would become my wife, and Mom attempted to broach the topic one morning during spring break.

"Is it serious with you and Barbara?" she asked nervously.

"Um, yeah," was the reply.

"Well, you didn't get that thing down there for stirring your tea, so be careful."

I had the mug in my hand but thought better of testing her theory. My face was red with embarrassment and there was a fair bit of resentment that the subject of sex was never brought up until now. Once I was out of the house and married, I swore I would create a household where no topic was off limits.

I guess it could have been worse. A few parents with teenage kids were at the bar the other night and one of them recalled his nightmare of birds and bees.

"My mother took me to Walgreens and made me buy condoms in the seventh grade," he said. "She brought me to her bedroom, took out a banana, and made me watch as she demonstrated how to use the rubber."

"Oh, my God!" gasped one of the women.

"It gets worse," he countered, holding up his hand. "To demonstrate why they made these things with a reservoir end, she poured milk into the condom."

That produced huge waves of laughter in the bar. He held up his hand in an attempt to hold the laughter until the end of the story.

"It gets worse," he said. "When the demonstration was over, she unrolled the condom, wiped the banana, unpeeled it, and ate it in front of me!"

He was right: it couldn't get any worse!

Twenty-four years and a stack of bills later, I have failed miserably in creating my own sexually expressed home. I was reminded of this shortcoming recently, when our new puppy was in heat. She was spotting blood around the house and hammering away at any stuffed animal that had the misfortune of crossing her path.

"What's going on with her?" asked the girls as she humped a hapless panda doll at our feet.

Here was my chance. The pooch could be a metaphor for the changes that would occur in their own bodies. I practiced this speech numerous times in my mind but when opportunity rose, I folded like a cheap chair.

"Um, it's a Mexican hat dance or something," I muttered, referencing the Chihuahua blood in our mixed breed. There was giddy laughter around the room. I loaded mariachi music on the iPod stereo nearby and we all got up and danced around the dog as she grinded on the plush toy at our feet. After the giggles subsided, my wife winked at me and I could see the wings of the birds and hear the buzz of the bees on the horizon.

I did what any repressed Irish Catholic man would do under the circumstances: I reached for the leash and took the dog for a walk. The pamphlet may have announced that my little girl was changing from a child to an adult, but in speaking openly on carnal matters, dear old Dad clearly had a lot of growing up to do.

A Modern Saint of the Church

As the Irish church sex abuse scandals tightened around the Vatican recently, I couldn't help but think how better communication could heal things. Once again, the old adage of the cover-up being worse than the crime was proven true.

I'd like to break with my journalistic colleagues' tradition of bashing the clergy for a moment in favor of sharing with you a story about communication of a different sort. It all started about a year ago, when I was enrolled in a course through Landmark Education titled Communication: Access to Power. When the facilitator asked us what we were hoping to get out of the weekend seminar, people shared how they wanted to have richer communication with loved ones and hoped to discover how to minimize conflicts with co-workers in the office, for example. We were all dying to know why the diminutive Irish American nun in the back of the room was attending the seminar and a hush came over the nondescript conference room as she approached the podium.

"My name is Sister Mary Elizabeth Lloyd; call me Sister Mary Beth," she said in a tone that barely registered above a whisper. This was a person clearly uneasy in the spotlight, her pale blue eyes darting nervously around the room without looking at any one person. "I am a Filippini nun and I'm trying to improve my negotiation skills."

The comment cocked many an eyebrow in the room; was this really some boardroom brawler in disguise, a titan of industry who would redden the knuckles of Donald Trump with a ruler until he begged for mercy? The instructor, sharing our amusement, used a slightly patronizing inflection to ask, "Sister, what do you negotiate?"

"I negotiate for the welfare of children," she replied, with a small, content smile. "My mission work takes me down to the bus stations of Brazil. Parents bring their little children down to the terminal so that visitors can rent them for sexual purposes. Some of these poor boys and girls aren't even 10 years old, yet working their children as prostitutes is the only means of support the family has.

"A group of us nuns visit the bus terminal and outbid the travelers. We pay the parents what they would make for an afternoon of the little child's time. We then take the boy or girl and play with them or buy them ice cream. So, I decided to take this course so that I can improve my negotiation skills and spend less money in my dealings so that I have more cash to reach more children."

The entire room swallowed the lumps in their throat in unison. The weekend course had many dinner breaks and we would sit open-mouthed as Sr. Mary Beth recounted the works done by the humble nuns of Filippini, who have been aiding the survival of the poorest children and women through charitable works for more than 300 years. This course had attendees of every race and creed, yet we all rooted for the Catholic nun, whose humility and selflessness was a model for all faiths. I was moved, touched, and inspired by her work with Child Headed Households (CHH), an organization that cares for children who have become head of their households after losing both parents to AIDS. She published her experience in a book, *AIDS Orphans Rising: What You Should Know and What You Can Do to Help Them Succeed*, which can be found on the website www. AIDSOrphansRising.org.

For the first time in decades, I was intensely proud of the clergy of my church and beamed as I reconsidered my Catholic nature once again. Though I went to Landmark's course to improve my leadership skills at work, I unexpectedly found myself resuming a long-forgotten conversation with God that we held during my halcyon days of frequent church attendance. When I opened my mind and heart to what was going on in Mass, instead of bringing my festering contempt for the collar into the house of God as I had been for the last 10 years, a funny thing happened. I was inspired to donate to worthwhile causes in the second collection: the retired clergy fund that helped with the medical bills of the dedicated priests and nuns who educated me in my formative years, the religious education foundation, and the mission work of modern-day saints like Sr. Mary Beth.

Palm Sunday marks the holiest week on our Catholic calendar, which makes the crucifixion of our church officials in the media ironic timing to say the least.

You may be tempted to send a message calling for change in our broken church by dialing down the Easter offering; I know I will. Consider taking that money you saved in the first collection and giving it to a worthwhile cause funded by the second collection. While most women her age are dyeing eggs with grandchildren, Sr. Mary Beth Lloyd and her colleagues are probably spending Easter working miracles in a Brazilian transit terminal with little more than the price of a bus fare. You can help by making checks payable to Religious Teachers of Filippini and mail to Sr. Mary Beth Lloyd, MPF at Villa Walsh, 455 Western Avenue, Morristown, NJ 07960.

A Catholic Cougar Looks to Prey

Perched atop a rustic bench in the snug of an Irish pub with a full pint at the end of a bent elbow in a tony suburban Orlando neighborhood, I was ready for what I thought might be the toughest writing assignment of my career.

My friend was dealing with a very lonely Irish mother-in-law and he was hoping to find her some company for the holidays. I was told that she was an extremely devout Catholic woman originally from Offlay who decided to set up shop on dating websites after a daughter and two girlfriends found love online and I was pitched as "the funny New York writer" who happened to be in town, and charged with composing a snappy profile that would attract Mr. Right.

She took a stab at writing about her ideal man and I rolled my eyes when I read in her e-mail about the blessings of her grandchildren and how she was "looking for a man who knows his place on this earth as a servant to our Lord." *Jesus, take the wheel, I have some work to do here!* While I was told she was well preserved and certainly could appreciate the beautiful daughter she created for my friend to marry, I was still expecting Susan Boyle's older ugly stepsister to walk in the door all the same.

My jaw dropped when I saw my friend and the impossibly curvaceous 67-year-old woman standing next to him. She had catlike eyes and a porcelain complexion that lurked beneath luxuriant waves of bleached blonde hair. Her alluring voice was roughed up by cigarettes and the brogue was fighting the good fight against a scuzzy southern drawl.

After a round of drinks, I expressed disbelief that she would be seeking companionship. In the course of an hour, the puzzle pieces started to fit.

47

Like so many of us, a ghost of some frigid grade-school nun was screeching in her ear about the sins of the flesh. You know the rap: sex is something not to be enjoyed, certainly not before marriage. After faithfully serving two deceased husbands and raising churchgoing adult children, I'm sure our charitable Maker would look the other way if this good woman rounded the bases of love in her last few innings.

Brides of Christ back in the day may have been excellent public servants and educators, but looking back, one can't help but think they were trying to stamp out sexuality with the same sensible shoes that stamped out their own. A nun like the one Meryl Streep played in *Doubt* educated me on the birds and the bees, and I still remember how her face looked like she had a wedge of rotten grapefruit in her gob as she described each sin in detail and what menu of punishments waited for us in Beelzebub's Buffet. To this day I see Sister in my head with a straw broom every time I have trouble brushing an impure thought away on my own.

I figured if we were going to hell for helping this active senior sin, we might as well have fun this evening, so I ordered another whiskey and began with my one-liners.

"Not looking for a man to turn loaves into fishes, but if you can raise the dead in bed, fair play to you!"

She gazed at her son-in-law with a look that said *I told you this wasn't a good idea*. I fretted with the fringes of my cocktail napkin nervously.

"OK, how about 'my list for the confessional is boring and I am looking for new sins to fry my friar'?"

She blessed herself and cackled.

"Jesus, Mary, and Joseph!"

Negotiations ensued that made Hilary Clinton's Pakistan trip look easy, but soon we were making considerable headway.

The liquor massaged our cerebella as the evening wore on. Before we got up and stumbled into the night air, I logged onto her account from my iPhone and uploading the following post to her profile page.

Catholic Cougar Looking to Prey

Are you tired of getting disappointed by lovers promising to turn water into wine? Yeah, I know the feeling. Good Irish Catholic woman looking for a reason to stay in bed on a Sunday morning, providing we make it to 5:30 Mass the night before. Seeking a clean guy older than the Son of God but younger than Abraham. Jesus is my ideal man, but kindly click your mouse somewhere else if you are 33, single, into piercings, and living with a mother who thinks you walk on water. Been there, done that.

I'm not looking for marriage, though it would be nice. I guess I'm just looking to turn a love life of Sorrowful Mysteries into something joyful. Wink if interested.

Rethinking Priests During the Year of the Priest

Now that I have to go to church every week if my eighth-grader has a chance of getting confirmed (oy vey!), I've been staring a lot at this banner announcing the "Year of the Priest" that hangs in our church. For those of you not in the know, Pope Benedict XVI declared a year for priests beginning with the Solemnity of the Sacred Heart of Jesus on June 19, 2009 and concluded in Rome with an international gathering of priests with the Holy Father June 9-11, 2010. This represents only 51 weeks, proving, as it turns out, the Pope is not infallible.

It brought me back to a time when every Irish mother dreamed that their son would be a priest; I know mine did. I remember well how Mom's blue eyes would dance when she was packing my bags for a school-sponsored religious retreat. "I think they see something in him," she might whisper to one of my aunts as the "men in black" came to collect me.

They saw something, all right. One of the clergy took a liking to me straight away. We would always have to stop and stay in a hotel on the way to our retreats and it was there that he would suggest we take off our shirts and wrestle to "get the tension out and give the old man a workout." To this day, I'm not entirely sure where his hands went during our tussle but now that I am a parent, I have come to gain a new level of awareness of what was going on. I also know that if a priest tried the same thing on one of my kids, I would have no problems blowing his head off and doing my time in the slammer.

My folks are amazing, devoted people who put the clergy on a pedestal and the idea of men betraying that kind of trust throughout our church while officials turned a blind eye fills me with an intense rage at times. That darkness flares up most Sundays, right around the time the church bells at the end of the altar boy's wrist shakes and announces our celebrant's arrival in the back of the building. It takes me most of the Mass to calm down and I wonder what the hell I'm doing there.

The church is losing members at an alarming rate, with most people now defining themselves as spiritual instead of practicing churchgoers. It would be easy to join those growing ranks, but then I look down at the example I set for my girls by being here, lose myself in the peace on the face of the Blessed Mother's statue, and try to push through those dark thoughts so that I can resume my communication with God.

I even attempted to purge those dark thoughts about all those abuse victims within the pages of *Collared,* my novel of suspense set in the church scandals published a few years ago. No surprise that the body count of clergy in those 382 pages ran preposterously high before any characters found redemption.

I'll never forget the signings in the days and weeks following the release of my book. I was expecting tweed-clad intellectualism at every turn like you see on Book TV, but those publicity stops turned into caustic town hall meetings about the betrayal of the flock by their shepherds and how we were all going to pick up the pieces. To inspire that rage and spirited dialogue is dreaming while awake for any writer trying to provoke, and that exchange of information is sorely missed during this Year of the Priest.

You may be thinking that I have an ax to grind against anyone wearing a collar—nothing could be further from the truth. I have since reconciled with that one misguided soul from my past and the countless hours of nurturing and pastoral care I experienced from the religious priests, brothers, and nuns in my youth provide for cherished memories.

I'm merely writing this as a plea for some frank dialogue about possibilities for the priesthood during the very time that the Pope has set aside for this institution. Celibacy is an antiquated mechanism that was intended to keep religious more devoted to their work, but we have seen evidence time and again in church documents and sordid lawsuits of how that vow attracted some warped souls unable to come to terms with their own denied sexuality.

I'm sure I'm not the only one in the congregation snickering when we greet our flamboyant celebrant with the opening hymn "Hail, Holy Queen." Please. Let's drop the pretense that gays should have no part in our ministry; without them we'd have very few men in the cloth and even fewer choir directors. Other religions have openly gay bishops and lo and behold, Satan's blood has yet to spout from the walls in those houses of worship. It's time to drop the "don't ask/don't tell" malarkey once and for all.

We need to explore the possibility of married priests who can set a meaningful example for those of us who elect the sacrament of matrimony and while we're at it, let's find a place for women that doesn't marginalize them to convents and delivering hosts to the sick on weekends.

Our church has a lot of challenges before it and I am a firm believer that every challenge is an opportunity ready to reveal itself. We need to do something to stem the tide of declining ordinations; Ireland was a hotbed for vocations in the past, which makes the recent headline in *The Irish Times* touting only 36 newly minted priests in that country so alarming.

During this Year of the Priest I hope we are all praying hard that we have the courage to transform this vocation into one that Irish mothers everywhere will want for their children once again.

God's Cheerleaders

I've just kissed my daughter on the cheek after drilling her on her Confirmation questions; I was shocked at how many of the answers I remember from my own Catholic rite of passage more than 30 years ago.

I've also never felt so distant from my faith. In fact, the last time I felt this way was about a year ago, when I was cradling my godson in my arms at the baptismal font. It seems these joyous times of marking significant events of our faith in my family's offspring forces me to tell the truth about myself and the unworkability of my personal relationship with the Catholic Church.

Sure, the scandals that have shaken our church to its core and my own inappropriate relationship with a clergyman in my teens have taken their toll on my faith. When I peel back the visible scar tissue, however, I see how my animosity goes much deeper than that.

Being Irish and Catholic meant a double whammy that produced just a trickle of joy in life during my formative years. If you were lucky to get your hands on a decent girl in high school, there was eternity in hell to pay if you died before confessing that sin next Saturday. Thanks to years of heavy-handed threats spun from misinterpretations of the *Baltimore Cathecism* in the Seventies by repressed clergy, you had barely lit the proverbial post-coital cigarette before you looked up in the heavens and pleaded for your Maker not to strike you down with a bolt of lightning before you were able to scrub the blackness of your soul.

As I get older, I move further away from the notion of living my life under constant threat of eternal damnation and as the head of this Catholic household, I wish a life for my kids that is not shackled with guilt as a constant way of being.

When you're not so busy making Mass on a Sunday morning, you can tune into what other faiths are offering these days. There is a part of me that is insanely jealous as I witness the inspiration, perspiration, and transformation emanating from the pulpits of the black churches on BET. Large women in silk hats waving handkerchiefs over their ample chests as they burn in their faith while men in mustard-colored suits whip the worshipers into a sweaty frenzy—who doesn't want in on that juicy conversation with the Lord? When was the last time a Catholic Mass galvanized you like that?

You don't even have to go that far over the edge to find peace and inspiration. Turn the dial and you find any number of these megawatt megachurch pastors who preach the power of positive thinking. Like lawyers, they make their case for a happy life by deftly weaving spiritual passages into sermons and presenting them as irrefutable proof that God wants us to be happy.

Against my better judgment, I can't help but be awed Joel Osteen's televised ministry, like a fascinated toddler. He's slick, sweet, and shiny, but I like what he says.

"God never created us to endure life," Osteen chirped from the stage recently. "He made us so that we enjoy life. He made us to be the happiest species on Earth. Some people go around with a long face. They go to church like they're going to a funeral!"

Wow! Did he ever nail the Irish Catholic church experience! If our priest runs his mouth and keeps us past 57 minutes, there is a palpable contempt in the pews that stops just shy of an outright palace coup. When you look at Osteen's crowd, you get the sense that they could hear his lighter-than-air sermons all day about the patient and loving father anxious to bestow heaven's bounties upon us.

I've also become a fan of Joyce Meyer, a more butch version of Osteen. A drill sergeant with sensible low heels that clack as she paces the stage, she seems mildly annoyed that we're ignorant of the Scripture and that God has cursed her with helmet hair. Like Osteen, she preaches positive thinking in a common-sense style of which I just cannot get enough.

She walks the walk as well. Fair play to her, she went through the mill: she talks openly about an abusive childhood and first marriage and has risen from the ashes to generate a ministry and speaking gigs that routinely fill hockey arenas each Sunday.

"Do you know you have a relationship with yourself?" she asked in a homily I picked up on YouTube. "You have a much more active relationship with yourself than anyone else. I mean, everywhere you go, there you are! Romans 12:2 says it clearly: 'Do not be conformed to this world, this age, fashioned after its external superficial customs.' If you don't change your mind, you are never gonna change your life. Proverbs 23:7 says, 'as a man thinketh in his mind so is he.' Amen."

Just when I "thinketh" I'm going to trade my Catholic hair shirt in for something else, I am stopped. Like a ring of scum in the bathtub, a certain Christian smugness has lined conservative culture in media like Fox News and Tea Party rallies that just turns my stomach.

I don't see myself as a promise-keeping kinda guy; I know a few of them and I hold their "Abercrombie & Christ" look in utter contempt. You know the type: he of sensible cardigan, soft-serve-yogurt hair, "WWJD" wrist band, JC and the Apostle sandals, and that certain pithy way he thinks the world should go according to Matthew, John, Paul, George, or Ringo.

Speaking of Beatles, I'll leave you with the gospel according to Sir Paul:

"When I find myself in times of trouble, mother Mary comes to me, speaking words of wisdom, let it be."

Despite the internal turmoil over my distance from regular Catholic communion, I still say a decade of the Rosary most days and I go around the beads many times during long car trips. I continue my prayers for the Blessed Mother's intercession to help me figure how to go in peace to love and serve the Lord.

Epilogue:

I took this letter into a confessional and read it to the priest. He apologized on behalf of his church and fellow priests. With that, all is forgiven on both sides. I went to church the next morning light of heart and present to God's goodness for the first time in twenty years.

Book 3: Living the Dream and Random Thoughts! Stout No More!

I'm not the kind who cries at the drop of the hat, but my eyes get positively dewy when I watch *The Biggest Loser*, the NBC smash-hit show that pits corpulent contestants against one another in a weight-loss challenge. The courage these folks exhibit taking off their shirts or stripping down to a sports bra and bike shorts on national television truly moves me. When they get to call home in exchange for winning a challenge that involves walking past a buffet table, I well up. When their toddler gets on the phone and says, "I love you" after being away from their parents during this fat camp stay, both contestant and viewer are reduced to a puddle of tears.

Yet in some cynical way, the show makes me feel better about myself: I thank God I haven't let myself go to that degree. Heck, I even admit to smirking at the fact that not one man on that show is sporting anything less than a "D" cup.

One evening, I laughed so hard at one person who had the circumference of a small moon orbiting Mars that I spilled my Venti Dulce de Leche Frappuccino Blended Crème all over my own man boobs. I paused, but those mammaries kept on with their carefree jiggling for a nanosecond longer. I swallowed hard on my mouth full of whipped cream. I looked down; nothing short of a dramatic life change or a full-on mastectomy could remove this coating of flab from my long buried pectorals. That's when I knew that there was no denying it any longer.

Sure, I saw the signs. Refusing to buy that next size, I purchased instead the Haggar Comfort Elastic waist trousers that were a size lower, choosing to bury the true numbers behind my escalating girth. "What are *you* doing in exercise clothes?" someone recently asked me at a business meeting as they passed me by on the walking trail. I'd look down in shame when I saw the discomfort on the faces of fellow air passengers as they pondered the possibility of me sitting next to them. I would hide from my wife in our walk-in closet, embarrassed to be seen huffing through nightly sock removal in broad daylight at the edge of the bed.

There was also denial at play in other areas. I could kid myself into thinking that old age was making my spine creak like old stairs when I reached around to wipe. *Oh, looky here! My arms are getting shorter, too!* I pretended that being on blood-pressure meds didn't bother me deeply. "This is a vitamin for my ticker," I replied to my daughter when she asked me why I took a pill with coffee every day. She left the exchange thinking Daddy was taking care of himself; I knew otherwise.

As long as I am letting it all hang out, I must confess to measured glee when everyone around me would fail in their own quest to lose weight. Like a NASCAR fan, I would sit on the sidelines rooting for the crash and burn. *She'll gain it all back and then some,* I would smirk underneath the smiles of support I threw my wife when she twirled around the house in a smaller size. Sorry, hon. Love ain't pretty when you've married a heartless, insincere buffet molester.

The New Year is all about turning the page of the calendar as one turns a new leaf, right? I am no exception. Like the majority of Americans, I kept a gym membership just to say I had a gym membership, and of course, I never went. Now I do. When a friend dropped a subtle hint and got me two months' membership for Christmas, I decided to turn that into two personal training lessons. I was taught how to exercise and, more importantly, how to change things up in my workout to keep it fun. I am happy to report that I am down 11 pounds in a little over 2 weeks! Let's focus on that and downplay the fact that if I just slim down to the weight my driver's license says I am, I will still be morbidly obese by some governmental standards.

The best thing I did with a Barnes & Noble gift card was to buy *Eat This, Not That,* a book by *Men's Health* Editor David Zinczenko. As the title suggests, it walks you through the pitfalls and payoffs of various menu choices in our favorite restaurants, buffet tables, and bars. Who knew a

McDonald's Quarter Pounder was a better choice at 493 calories/19g of fat when compared to the Wendy's Roasted Turkey and Swiss Frescata with small fries (1100 calories/40g fat). A factoid that made my day was that a pint of Guinness Draught, whose dark and heavy aura would lead some to believe it to be a meal in a glass, was in the "light beer" category at only 128 calories! Our God is good. Interestingly and inexplicably, the Guinness Extra Stout has 176 calories.

With the right choices and a new commitment to my health, I will be getting rid of the stout in more ways than one. Wish me luck!

Seventeen down, thirty more to go! I am one third of the way to realizing a New Year's resolution that everyone around me was convinced would have a shelf life shorter than milk.

I just got back from taking my Chihuahua-pug mix (or "Chug" for short—an appropriate breed for an Irish music writer if ever there were one) to the vet, who informed me that she is sixteen pounds. I briefly thought about stapling her to my ass to get the true feeling of hauling that much weight around, but I thought better of it and opted instead to curl her under my arm as I ran up the stairs twice. I was so winded! I couldn't imagine walking around with that gravitational pull at work on me at all times, but that is exactly how I was living before I got serious about losing weight.

This healthy journey these last six weeks has been full of dizzying highs and the lowest of lows.

I am amazed at the blinding discipline that has come out of nowhere and has this fleshy ass in the gym almost every day; there are small, budding fruits for my labor. Each week brings a new distance record on the treadmill and another notch lower on the weight machines. Hard baseballs pop under my skin as I flex my arm muscles. I have been talked out of the "X" in front of "XL" in most sizes. My blood pressure medicine has always been pushed to its upper limits, but now it is keeping my rate at normal ranges.

I think I might have found my inner chin! It is beginning to jut out ever so slightly from the bib o' chub that has gathered around my neck. Like a groundhog, it threatens to retreat if it sees its shadow or another Grande Caramel Macchiato.

Speaking of, I have narrowly avoided the near occasion of dietary sin at Starbucks, opting instead for the skinny latte. Sure the milk doesn't froth quite the same without the fat in it, but it sure beats ordering a Plavix smoothie from my cardiologist's juice bar in a few years. I've said good-bye to the McGriddle, that slice of breakfast heaven in between two syrup infused faux pancakes; I now settle on a protein-laden Zone Bar with my coffee instead.

I am most proud of my killer rack! My man boobs have been stretched on a bed of new pectoral muscles, shrinking the elongated, saggy pooch ta-tas to a perky C cup that would make a Rodeo Drive high school girl text her plastic surgeon with envy.

Sure, there have been breakdowns. I ate the equivalent of my own body weight in hash browns and steak during a bachelor party a few weeks ago. I have taken the dare of "Betcha can't eat just one" off the bag of Lay's and have lost miserably, shoveling them into my mouth by the handful during, ironically enough, *The Biggest Loser*.

Not since Jesus sweated it out in the garden of Gethsemane has a man doubted himself with such zeal. A few weeks ago, my body plateaued at an unlucky 13- pound weight loss for three weeks. They say you should only weigh yourself once a week, but I hopped on the scale constantly during this period: following a shave, before and after eliminating my body of all solid and liquid waste, and always naked. When I treaded water like this, I actually had to back away from a box of laxatives in the medicine cabinet. *Lord, thy will be done, make me lose the weight without the runs. Amen.*

Thank God for the flu pandemic going around last week; I felt like hell but I was willing to do anything to break my stalemate. Three pounds lost!

Along the road to wellness, I have descended into the hellish cul-de-sac of food nightmares. Four Girl Scout Thin Mints have chased my car in perfect formation. I have been pinned in a corner, a red licorice whip and folding chair keeping me from three tiger-shaped animal crackers. Or I am running for my life as a giant rolling Ring Ding chews the lawn and gains precious ground behind me.

Not even my naughty night fantasies are safe. I am ashamed to admit that I have a crush on Britney Spears; there is something about that single-mom white-trash look of hers that melts my butter (or, in this case, Smart

Balance trans-fat-free buttery spread) because you just *know* she would join in any reindeer games for a scratch-off and a pack of unfiltered Camels. Anyway, the other night I am frothing my own beer thinking about the two of us in the back of her limo. The car comes to a stop right before Britney rolls down the window and orders popcorn chicken at KFC. As we resume the nasty necking, my eyes can't help but move away from her overstuffed bustier and onto the grease stains that bleed through the face of "The Colonel" on the bag in her hand.

I'm just starting to have people compliment me on my weight loss, a critical component if this acknowledgment whore hopes to burn his expandable waist pants in effigy. There aren't enough people noticing that I am 17 pounds lighter, however, which is a troubling indicator of just how fat I am if nearly twenty pounds lost looks like a daisy in a bull's mouth.

Am I really that shallow and vain? You bet. But I know I am playing for a lot more. I am playing for my life and the lives of my children. This is a marathon, not a sprint, and I will just keep power-walking my way to a new me!

I made the mistake of announcing to my daughters that we would all be going to Ireland once I lost 40 pounds and now they're all over me. It's galling to be coached away from the Doritos by an 11-year-old, but I am willing to take any help I can get. With three women on my case, we will be on the auld sod in no time!

Besides, I've got this sick little fantasy of flipping a two-fisted bird to a certain aunt who purses her lips and says, "Jaysis, yeh got heavy" as soon as I deplane. Sometimes, it's the only thing keeping me going during spinning sessions.

Other little scenarios motivate me. Like I bought this decadent animal-print terrycloth robe at a boutique hotel in Boston recently and I am deathly afraid of wearing it outside for a few steps to get the paper. I live next door to a state trooper who is obsessed with hunting, and I fear that he will mistake me for a cheetah taking down a water buffalo if he is groggy at the window as I bend over to fetch the *Times*. If I lose this weight, I just know he will think twice before aiming at a lithe panther! Though I have never felt better or more confident in my determination to maintain a healthy lifestyle, I live in almost constant fear of a stray Twinkie acting as the lone gunman on the grassy knoll that knocks me off the Skinny Limo. I am mindful of the copious Guinness intake this week and know I will be choosing between stout and food, which is the classic sign of a drunkorexic. Pray for me. The eyes are open and the mouth stays shut. Stay tuned.

Epilogue:

One year later, I have gained back all but seven pounds of what I lost after writing this article. I purposefully folded all of the skinny clothes I had bought before going into the attic's crawl space to get the jumbo Tupperware full of fat clothes I thought I had packed for good. I was chagrined to find the following note I had written to myself fourteen months earlier taped to the lid of the container.

10/5/09

You Fat Fuck.

Something told me you'd be reaching for these clothes again. I knew it. You knew it, too. Otherwise, you would have given these tents with buttons and zippers to charity. At some level, you knew you'd need them again.

I mean, really. You couldn't back away from the buffet table, could you? You have all the willpower of a pedophile in a playground and that makes me sick.

You were doing so well for a while there. Using that calorie counter app on your iPhone, going to the gym on a regular basis, all of that shit. You were on the right track for a while there and you actually seemed to be turning a page on a long chapter of food addiction and laziness that has been your life. Heck, you had me going there for a while and you know you can't fool your inner voice easily. I know you better than anyone else.

You had the eye of the tiger when you wrote that article about getting thin to the readers of *The Irish Voice* and now you have the eye--and ass—of the hippopotamus. What happened?

I can't believe you're reaching for the XXL Banana Republic V-neck black sweater that's in here. You actually conned yourself into thinking that this look would be slimming on you when you bought it. You think you can really hide those C-cup tits under a black piece of cashmere and a blazer that's bigger than the mast of the Cutty Sark? Think again.

This container is located in the attic, just over your bed. Or at least, that's where you used to sleep.

How many times have you actually *slept* in there since putting the weight back on? The fat around your windpipe produces a snoring that sounds like two mastodons getting it on. Are you really getting a good night's sleep on the futon in the guest room? Please tell me you've stopped making Barb wrong for waking you up in the middle of the night.

You had a goal in mind to get off the blood pressure medicine once you hit your ideal weight. Remember that? Who knows how fat you are now? You might as well throw Plavix and Metformin into the blender, and with the Diovan and a dollop of skim milk, make yourself a heart attack prevention smoothie. Jesus, you make me sick.

Heel spurs, double chins, back spasms. All signs you choose to avoid. Well, keep pouncing on Ben & Jerry's like Whitney Houston on a rock of crack, fat boy, and the clothes in this container might become your skinny clothes. Imagine that.

With kind regards,

Your Inner Voice

Epilogue II

It's November 2010 and I am down 12 more pounds. There is hope for me yet.

Goodbye, Goatee!

In reading over some of these essays, I have been troubled by how many words were devoted to my poor self-image.

That's it!

Your lard arse is going to the gym once and for all, I thought to myself. Since then, I have been a dervish of activity in the cause of my own health! All egg whites and portion controlled proteins and greens for me, thank you very much! I have been squeezing every drop out of this indian summer we had over the weekend and I suited up the sneakers for workouts most days. Twelve pounds have come off in a short period of time, but it isn't fast enough for my liking.

To speed the process up some and to capitalize on this self-loathing, I did the unthinkable: I took a blade to my chin and shaved off the goatee I have been wearing for the last thirteen years. It was hiding the lies about the bib o'chub and I literally couldn't stare it in the face any longer!

But that wasn't even the most radical piece of this! I loaded a yoga mat into the back trunk and joined my wife for a class in an attempt to tone up for the book tour. After an hour of pretzel contortions while mechanical birds chirped in the loudspeaker, I put in a workout more severe than anything a drill sergeant could dish out. Hey, if it worked for Sting, it would work for me!

So, I set off on a brilliantly sunny day last Friday to do publicity shots and book jacket photos because the artwork is due on Monday. I posted the pictures on my Facebook account and even took the "before and after shots" to the pub for the lads to help decide which look to go with.

Remind me to never do that again, please!

"It's feckin' facial hair, for the love of God," said one paddy, rolling his eyes to the heavens as his short block fingers teased his widow's peak. He placed the pictures on the bar, careful to dip them into the ring of moisture left by his pint glass, and motioned to the bartender. "Can you get 'Michele' over here a whiskey please? She's a bit parched after going to her yoga class. Put some Pogues on the jukebox while yer at it---her poor head is probably still ringing with that Enya nonsense."

"Yeh better make that a pint of water," shouted Seamus as he grabbed the pictures. "Yeh might as well put a tinkle of vinegar into the glass as well, in case yer man over here needs a douche!"

I didn't take a bit of notice of this and took it for what it was: a jealous, curt comment from a friend of mine who hides a desire to be a comedian and actor behind the brick walls he builds around Tarrytown. With his wooly bleached hair, translucent eyes, and bushy eyebrows that seem to brush in any hint of mayhem into his thick skull, this native Dubliner just might hit the stage sooner rather than later!

"Yerra, I'm still not sure I like the clean-shaven look," he sighed dramatically. "Why did you cut it off again?"

"I was tired of hiding behind it," says I. "I realized the goatee was hiding the double chins and all of the bad health and poor lifestyle choices that went with it over the years and I am turning over a new leaf."

"Good onya, boyo," he replied, rubbing my shoulders with ham hands and a vice grip. "Mind yeh, I think the whole goatee of yours was like puttin' a f*cking rosebush in front of a wall of grafitti---I mean, who we kiddin' here?"

American Idol contestants have it easy compared to the judges I have to put up with in my watering hole. Perhaps I might want to hang with my yoga gals a bit more; they're too kind to judge me, even in my spandex.

Namaste!

A Masculinity Makeover
at the Home Depot

"What are you doing this weekend?" asked one of my friends during a couples' night out.

"We're refinishing the hardwood floors," came my reply.

"Are you doing it yourself?"

My wife let out a laugh before I could reply; it was an extended chuckle that went on a little too long for my liking.

It's no accident I called this column "The Narrowbacks Corner." According to the Urban.com dictionary, a *narrowback* is a child of Irish immigrants who is considered too soft to do hard physical labor. Used in a sentence: "You narrowbacks would never make it in the old country. You don't know what hard work is."

Yup, guilty as charged.

My wife had every reason to laugh because I am so useless around the house that the very thought of me operating a sander to repair a scuffed floor is as unlikely as Whitney Houston passing by a crack house on her way to church.

Though he probably would never admit it, I'm sure my father has considered getting a paternity test on many occasions over the years to make sure I was indeed sired from his loins, because we couldn't be more different. He is a workman, living off the Athenry soil before crossing the pond to fend for himself as a roofer and factory worker. He has thick, callused hands and broad shoulders to show for decades of hard labor.

He'd sometimes bring me along in a feeble attempt to teach me how to work with wood, nails, or wiring. It was no use. Before long, he'd proclaim me to be the "feckin' eejit" that I was/am. Soon I would be banished to some marginal job as a flashlight holder or a tool handler, only to look over his shoulder, dejected and emasculated, while he hovered over the project at hand.

Those feelings of inadequacy from my teenage years always flare up whenever I walk into a Home Depot. I was there this weekend to run an errand in an attempt to make myself useful while contractors worked on those hardwood floors. I was sent to find plastic discs to place under the legs of my tables and chairs because God forbid we scuff the floors and ruin the work of the real men that I paid to do what I cannot! With my board shorts and flip-flops, I could feel my reproductive organs alter like some earthworm as I walk past rough-hewn men scanning the aisles with their steel-toed boots and tool belts jangling against each hip. The fact that this transformation occurs in the middle of the plumbing aisle is not lost on me. I hide my shame behind the display of area rugs, which is nestled within the girly section of the store that contractors call the painting and decorating department. I feel like Hilary Clinton at a Limbaugh family reunion as I check out; these plastic discs might as well be a tube of lip gloss as I scan the drill bits and sandpaper in the carts of the men around me.

In fact, as I type this, my leg is wrapped in bandages and propped on a pillow after a home-improvement project that went horribly wrong over the weekend.

Writing is such a nancy-boy profession that it is perfect for a flaming narrowback like myself when you think about it. Someone pays you to prattle on about your poor tortured life, mining the minutiae of your ordinary Irish upbringing for some witty observation that most men either rarely notice or never think about. The worst that can happen in this line of work involves some editor sending you back to your desk in tears over an errant comma.

I guess I shouldn't complain. It will take me about twenty minutes to write this drivel and for the effort, I will be paid the equivalent wage of a day laborer in a Nike sweatshop without breaking said sweat. I am the one who gets dispatched to a bar and I must soak up drinks on the tab of my wife's hot friend when she is looking to punch up a Match.com profile after yet another thug breaks her heart. And when the economy turned downward last year, my friends in the construction business were lining up at the door of yours truly for a resume remodeling, proving once again that the pen is mightier than that sword—or that thingamabob that drives nails into wood.

Irish Pimpin'

Ladies, my Mercedes/Hold fo' in the back, two if it's fat/Keep a gat, for cats that try to test me/don't know what you heard about me

That Notorious B.I.G. He's a sage. Isn't there something so cool about being a gangsta pimp? What Irish guy doesn't dream of that life?

I know. A pudgy 44-year-old Irish guy doesn't have the swagger or the big hand to slap any 'ho' in line, but Michael Keaton was one of the most memorable agents of the flesh in 1982's *Night Shift*, so there you go. It gives us Celtic aspiring pimps some hope.

I don't know if I will ever have what it takes, but I do know that one of the downstream effects of having to drive secondhand American cars over the years is that you do spend a bit more on nicer rides once you have a few nickels to rub together.

Uh-huh. Pimp cars.

This morning I am contemplating my next mac daddy ride because the lease of my Cadillac CTS is up.

In the same way you call an Irishman to find the best bar to abuse your liver in Manhattan, I called one of my African American friends from Bedford Stuyvesant to get his advice on my next pimp-mobile.

Steve is actually a renaissance man and a personal hero of mine who rose from dire circumstances to create a thriving digital advertising firm. We both have island relatives; mine are from Ireland and his are from Barbados. It was in some dimly lit Irish bar that he acknowledged our connection and christened himself Dark Pint.

"So, I have been looking at some pimp-able cars," I said. "We got us a list of cars I can afford and I've done some online research. Can I run some by you?"

"Go ahead," came Dark Pint's reply.

The BMW 328xi. "That is a pimp car," he said. "But it's like a soccer mom pimp, the kind of housewife that runs her stable out of the gals in her carpool. It's for the pimp that's packing a tampon instead of a gat, if you catch my drift."

I nodded my head and smiled knowingly. Clearly, I came to the right place for advice.

The Volvo XC60? "That's a bit better, but not by much," he declared with not a small measure of authority. "The pimp with this ride is socially conscious. He's gonna smack his girl around a bit, just like everyone else, but when he's done, he's gonna extend his hand, lift her up, and dust her off. Hell, he might even crawl on the floor and help her look for the missing tooth in the carpet."

The Mercedes GLK350? "Now we're talkin'," Dark Pint replied enthusiastically. "This says 'I know I'm a pimp, you know I'm a pimp, but some fake playa that writes for an Irish newspaper doesn't quite know the extent of my pimpness.' Any Mercedes model is gonna say that. I think it's a lot more pimpin' than that poseur Cadillac CTS you're drivin' now. I mean, that's like the green garbage they sell at Irish festivals. It's just this cartoon sh*t that passes off as Irish. Am I understood?"

I understand. I also understand the love of a Cadillac that is in my genes. It's an immigrant's way to show the world he made it in this new land.

I remember my father's first Caddy. As memory serves, it was a white Coupe DeVille, with fins and a trunk that was the size of a one-bedroom apartment. The front of the car got to your destination a full ten seconds before you did, or at least that's the way it seemed to the 8-year-old in the back seat.

Of course, we didn't get the car until 1974, years after it initially rolled off the assembly line. It was on its last legs by the time my dad held the title, but I remember his pride in owning it. He lined the family in front of it one morning, snapped a picture, and sent it home to his mother in Ballyglunin.

Mind you, he did this not to be boastful, because Herself would not tolerate it. Rather, he mailed the photo as assurance that her son was surviving and thriving in this new land and she could stop worrying and wringing her bony hands by the turf fire. It was proof positive that thanks to hard work and overtime pay, her son was keeping his Athenry pimp hand strong in Jersey City.

After all's said and done, I will probably buy the Caddy lease out. I guess Method Man got it right:

This pimpin that I got in my blood/It came from a family tree/My granddaddy was a pimp, my great great GREAT granddaddy was a pimp!

The Uncle I Hardly Knew

There's a picture of my Uncle Bobby taken at Christmastime forty-some years ago. He had just come over from Ireland and was looking down adoringly at the baby lying on his lap, the wide grin on his face indicating he was scarcely able to believe that he was an uncle.

The baby in the picture was me and that image was what flashed inside my eyelids as I rubbed my temples in prayer over his coffin.

This isn't going to be a eulogy about Bobby Cleary, as I am unqualified to write about the man. I saw him at family gatherings here and there over the years, but the conversation rarely moved beyond small talk and little in the way of a significant connection existed between the two of us. As the relationship between him and my mother—his sister—ebbed and flowed over the years, as it does in almost every Irish family, I maintained a safe distance on the shoreline.

Social networking has transformed many of the ways we relate to one another, and the Irish wake is no exception. A Facebook page was erected in his memory within hours of his passing and friends of my cousins immediately joined his children in a flurry of posts, little pieces of a jigsaw puzzle strung together to create a full picture of a beloved man from every angle. His teenage grandkids howled in anguish, his kids pledged eternal devotion to a man who made them what they are today, and friends recalled a gentle soul that always made them smile. The cursor blinked in the comment box, trying to coax the one writer in the family into saying a word or two, but nothing came. It made me felt awkward and ashamed that people who had none of his blood through their veins knew him and loved him more than I did.

The air in the funeral parlor was heavy with sugary pollen from the flowers as music from his beloved Simon & Garfunkel and Woody Guthrie played quietly in the background. There was a hush in the room before Dawn Mulvihill, his loving partner of many years, poured every ounce of suffering and heartbreak she had into the mournful melodies that wafted from her violin. I made my way over to the table filled with memorabilia near his coffin; a banjo case next to his beloved *New York Post* (dated on the day of his death) rolled into a tight tube and snapshots of the man and his family at various stages of our lives. There were drawings from his smaller grandchildren of crayon stick figures bent in inconsolable grief, spewing blue tears as a perfectly round sun shone at the left hand corner of the page. A weathered banjo was propped up in the middle of it all; my mother touched my shoulder, leaned in, and whispered, "He made that, you know."

The neck and fingerboard were well worn; the head was yellowed and ornately decorated with his painted artwork. I squinted to read the small inscription scrawled underneath the green Gaelic knots and it read, "Nationality is a jewel to be preserved at all peril." A quote from Irish political activist and writer Pádraig Pearse, it made me swallow hard.

In July 1914, Pearse was made a member of the Supreme Council of the Irish Republican Brotherhood (IRB), a militant group that believed in using force to throw the British out of Ireland. Though I never picked up a brick and hurled it at one of the Crown's tanks, I've always thought of my weekly column as a small contribution that keeps our nationality and culture alive in the same way (though not nearly as eloquently) that my hero Pearse did with his writings. The love of music, sense of family, and admiration of cultural icons like Pádraig Pearse provided indisputable evidence that I had lost a kindred spirit in my Uncle Bob, and I was intensely sad that the opportunity to know and love him more deeply slipped through my fingers.

The frigid wind at his burial site eventually blew us down the hill and into the church hall for lunch. Bob's old friend, Mike Ward, strapped on an accordion and joined Dawn to create a right Irish hooley and the mood soon lightened for everyone but me. Bob would have been proud to see how he had passed down a love of music and culture to this branch of the family tree, with each one of them taking a turn at the mike. My cousin Rob was hunched over an acoustic guitar as his sister Georgiana sang U2 tunes beautifully. The words of "Bad" ended the cycle of regret and self-pity in which I found myself that day.

This desperation

Dislocation

Separation

Revelation

Isolation

Desolation

Let it go and so fade away.

Rest in peace, Bob. Save me that stool next to yours at the great bar in the sky, as I am looking forward to making up for lost time.

"You Have an Answer for Everything!"

I have heard that rejoinder many times in my life in various ways: it has been said to me through gritted teeth with fists balled to the side of my opponent (*Hi, honey!*) at the conclusion of an argument just as many times as it has been produced while the other's head shakes from side to side, grudging admiration escaping through a wry smile.

Isn't that our job as Irish people, to be quick with the lucky charms? Isn't it in our genetic code to have a witty comeback at the ready?

There are lightning-quick jousts in the coliseum of corporate America, where I have plied my trade in sales leadership for too many years to mention, and I am eternally grateful to count the tongue as an arrow in my quiver. I recall one sticky human-resources situation not long ago, when I inherited an aging African-American woman in my roster when I began a new role. I looked over her dismal sales numbers over the last half of a decade and asked why she was still around.

"Let's just say her demographics make her hard to terminate," came the reply from the owner. "And don't think she won't remind you." I collected my data and met her in the conference room with a 90-day written warning that gave her two options: improve or ease on down the road.

"Mike, this isn't a black and white issue, is it?" she asked, fingering the sides of the document with the seductive smile of a spider greeting a fly in her web.

I am a person who thinks that greatness and incompetence have one thing in common: they are blind to color, race, and creed. Having my character assaulted brought my blood to a rolling boil instantly. "Actually, it is a black or white issue," said I. "You either made your number or you didn't, and clearly, you didn't. Seems black and white to me. What are you implying?"

She blinked as a thin layer of perspiration gathered above her lip line. Thanks to quick Irish thinking, this spider would have to find a new fly to make a meal of as she was looking for a new job.

Of course, the swift thinking doesn't always allow for weighing words, as poor Ronan Tynan discovered during a very public misunderstanding of an ill-placed joke that unfairly tarred the accomplished vocalist as a racist in the New York gossip columns not long ago.

Being too clever for one's own good has been my downfall once in a while. I remember being a 16-year-old with a big mouth that even the steel cage of braces could not contain. I was working the lottery machine and cash register at the local pharmacy and one of our regular customers came in. "Big Al" waddled down the aisle to the pharmacist's desk, chomping on a soggy, unlit cigar that rolled around his mouth like a fresh turd. He was here for his monthly shipment of Cuban cigars, smuggled in on his behalf and dispensed with his many medications at the back register. He struck a match halfway down the aisle and a puff of smoke trailed him as he walked toward the cash register.

"Mr. Lowenberg, you can't smoke that in here," I said, impressed with my authoritative tone and hoping the cute cashier at the other register was catching this.

"Oh, really?" he replied. "Listen you f***ng punk, I bought the thing here and I am gonna smoke it here!"

"Well, thank God for us all you didn't buy a laxative, sir."

With that, I got the girl. She laughed out loud, which inadvertently amplified the public humiliation of Big Al. He promptly summoned the owner, who fired me on the spot. Sure, it was a killer line that still gets a huge laugh when I tell the story almost 30 years later, but the smart-aleck remark cost me my favorite job and I do remember a painfully long bike ride home wondering how I was going to make money for a car.

Being a father, I now encourage my girls to be more respectful of elders than their father was. I am thrilled to report that they know their place, and their maturity leaves this proud dad who has an answer for everything speechless at times!

Work on St. Patrick's Day? Nunsense!

The creaky voice over the intercom made me freeze in terror. "Would Michael Farragher please come to the principal's office?"

It was the morning of March 17, 1972, and I was head down and minding my own business in kindergarten, probably hacking my way through construction paper with plastic scissors at the time the call came. Small knees knocked and the little bladder worked overtime as I took the long walk and stood in front of the smoked-glass door of Sister Mary Regina's office. Were those the anguished squeals of children being tortured in the next room or was it just her sensible shoes squeaking on the other side of the glass?

She opened the door and I came face to face with the star of many a nightmare. Dyed red hair was sculpted under a blue veil and in the middle of her thin, parched face were piercing blue eyes magnified by thick glasses. Upperclassmen warned me that the goggles actually amplified her laser vision, which came in handy as she burned your soul on the way to hell. Did I mention that the little bladder was working overtime at this point?

"Your name Farragher?" she snorted.

"Yes, Sister," I stammered.

"You don't ever go to school or work on St. Patrick's Day ever again. Do I make myself perfectly clear?"

"Yes, Sister," came the reply.

"Good. I'm sending you home."

This has set off a chain reaction of celebrations ever since, as you can imagine. While I can't vouch for my school attendance after I transferred out of St. Anne's in Jersey City, I know that everything came to a stop during my college and work years each March 17. When you have 24 hours to get into trouble, trouble will find you to be sure. Like many Irish folks, I have my share of drinking stories that have become the stuff of legend among friends and coworkers. There was the time 15 years ago when the technical director of my firm flew into LaGuardia on that day to see a big client in the morning and he was eager to see the famed New York parade. He was British and complained loudly about how the Irish got all the credit for being Europe's biggest drinkers when it was really the Queen's subjects who were superior. Of course, he said it loudly enough that myself and a number of others along the parade route took the bait. When I finally came to, at the not-so-gentle prodding of the train conductor, I had slept through my stop and three others, with no sign of my colleague. We barely made it to the presentation the following morning, each one of us repeatedly excusing ourselves to dry heave into the john just outside the conference room. The story of how a good friend extricated me from the prying paws of an Irish drag queen who called herself "Lady Gay-lick" outside Pat O'Brien's in the French Quarter on another March 17 is something I'll leave to your able imaginations.

My decadent behavior during those years certainly didn't help my mother's efforts to improve our national image. She would faithfully write to the Hallmark card company every year in protest over the portrayal of the Irish as drunks in their green greetings. Though I thought she was stark raving mad at the time, my view of our holiday is more in line with my mother's nowadays. Sure, I'll still hoist a pint or two, but my first stop is now a church, where I reflect on the saint who was captured and carried off as a slave to Ireland in his teens. After remaining captive for six years as a herdsman, his faith grew daily and when he escaped back to Roman Britain, he recalls a haunting vision. "I saw a man coming, as it were from Ireland," he wrote. "His name was Victoricus, and he carried many letters, and he gave me one of them. I read the heading: 'The Voice of the Irish.' As I began the letter, I imagined in that moment that I heard the voice of those very people who were near the wood of Foclut, which is beside the western sea—and they cried out, as with one voice: "we appeal to you, holy servant boy, to come and walk among us."

Is it any wonder that Patrick is our patron saint? His lesson is one that many Irish and Irish Americans here in the States can identify with: you may leave Ireland, but Ireland never leaves you. Sr. Regina knew that, and when I am in church on the morning of St. Patrick's Day, I will light a candle and thank that nun for watching over my wretched soul and instilling a sense of Irish pride in my formative years.

Playing Ketchup with Granny

Although I was born in Jersey City, there is something about the fork in the road on the N17 on the way to my grandmother's house in Ballyglunin near Athenry that tells me I've arrived home. Accompany me on this.

You are loath to buy into reincarnation, but there is an undeniable sense of silent company walking with you down a hill on the thin tongue of blacktop between Uncle Matty's house and your grandmother's place next door. The hills that your grandfather worked and so suddenly died upon are a green patchwork, with cobblestone fences dividing the fields from our neighbors.

You can hear the soft murmur of the livestock braying at either side of you and lambs calling out for their mothers as dusk settles. A rickety car makes its way toward you and a man you do not know waves his hand in greeting anyway. That's the kind of people who live here. The smell of the bog belches out of the chimney in soft black puffs, telling you that Granny Farragher has lit the turf fire and it is time for dinner.

You walk in and there is a weathered table on your right. There is butter and crumbs from the morning's bread where "herself" would have sat, her hawkish blue eyes devouring the contents of the newspaper that lies folded near the mug of tea. Sensing you are judging the dirty dish, she calls for you to come into the parlor.

She is there, her hair an impossible shade of brownish red that is pulled back into a hard bun. She tried going to her natural color once and when she saw pictures of the gray hair at 87 she exclaimed, "Jaysis, who is that old woman staring me in the face!" before quickly dyeing it again.

Her thin frame is perpetually in motion, contained within a thick blue apron of a dress that she wears regardless of the weather. She smokes half of an unfiltered cigarette, the other part of the "fag" with the filter in the top drawer because it is her way of only smoking half of what she used to.

With a knowing glance here and a head gesture over there, she directs the aunts in putting out the big spread without ever saying a word.

Irish ham, cold cuts, and cheeses are rolled up into tight logs, fanned out on the plate like spokes on a wheel. In the center of each dish is a perfectly symmetrical tomato and a yellow potato salad, homemade of course. Mugs of tea and high glasses of orange soda are never allowed to go below half full, thanks to the wordless nods of the head by Herself.

"Tell me about your life in America," she would say, her bony hand taking yours as her intense eyes are magnified through thick smudged bifocals. You prattle on about your good grades in school, the minor victories you have had at sports, and the great essays you've written in English classes.

"He is good-looking and modest," she would say through pursed lips. It's not until later that you realize her sharp tongue and intellect have dissected you and put those boastful ways in their proper place.

"Do you have everything you need, pet?" she would ask, proudly surveying the spread that has been put out before you.

"I didn't see any ketchup, Granny. Do you have any lying around?"

An eyebrow is raised, a head is tilted, and the uncle's wife is dispatched to make the five-mile ride into Tuam.

"Well, God blast yeh," she says, half-laughing. "Sure, the Lord Jesus Christ could cook the Last Supper with His own two hands and this Yank'd ask for the ketchup."

The ketchup would be at every meal from that point forward, even if it was toast being served, just to prove that you'll never catch her flat-footed again.

The suitcase is packed, tears are shed, and a few hundred Irish pounds are crumpled and placed in your palm. You smooth them out in the backseat on the way to the airport and soon realize that there is the equivalent of your father's weekly wage in your hand.

The most valuable gift, however, is revealed when you open your suitcase and find a one-liter bottle of Kandee Great Value Family Pack Tomato Ketchup as a memento of your dinner. There is a note taped to the bottle. "Now if you are without ketchup it's your own fault."

From that point forward until the woman's death, you will bring her a bottle of Heinz as a souvenir from America. She will shrug, shake her head, lift her eyes to the heavens, and laugh with a rattled cough before stabbing her turf fire with a spike.

You lean into her hospital bed to give her a kiss for the last time, her lungs filling up with water by the second. The woman in the bed next to her is wailing out to no one in particular, lost in her own madness. Your grandmother bristles for a second and between labored breaths says, "Sure, I wouldn't be in here a'tall if I had her lung power."

When you open your suitcase in your bedroom after making the trip home from her house, you will find packets of ketchup in your shirt collar, pants pocket, and medicine bag.

You will take that liter ketchup bottle into every apartment or house that you will call home from now on, the red container producing a smile each time you look at it. It makes you think back on the life of an amazing woman and provides a past connection of your own sly sense of humor and the obsession with always getting the last word, which in this Irish woman's case translates into "Remember me."

Music Knows No Boundaries

Ev'rything's free and easy/Do as you darn well pleasey/Why don't you make your way there/Go there, stay there/Once you get down Lambeth way/Ev'ry evening, ev'ry day/You'll find yourself doin' the Lambeth walk.

I swear on a stack of bibles I do not listen to show tunes! Sometimes they slap me in the face when I turn on the ignition of my wife's car because she has our Sirius satellite radio permanently turned to the Broadway channel! Honest!

I usually rush to switch the dial even before the engine turns over, but I left "The Lambeth Walk" from *The Music Man* for a few seconds because it was my grandmother's favorite song and it brought back great memories of her.

She had a high-pitched speaking voice that morphed into a pleasant hum when she busied herself with chores around her modest cottage. It was the kind of high voice that made you feel warm inside, which was the same effect her radiant smile and mischievous wink might have on you. It wasn't a powerful instrument but the voice would fill the room with escalating octaves, like Snow White's in the grainy early Disney cartoons.

Her house was nestled in an overgrown thatch of nettles and trees mere feet away from a treacherous curve in the small road. Blink and you miss it, and that would be a shame because the small garden in front of the door was immaculately maintained and a sight to behold.

Most weekends she would walk about a quarter mile to the crossroads, and wave when she saw Mrs. Sampson coming. She might have been the only one of Granny's friends with a car at the time.

They would always call one another "missus," their unlikely friendship born out of a mutual love of church music. Knowing Granny, she would probably sneak discreet glances at the big hat and white gloves Missus was wearing, too focused on how her simple flowered dress looked next to those fine clothes to be envious.

Missus would have had running spring water throughout the pipes of her house. It would take my grandfather years to dig trenches through his fields and run a pipe from the same well. Granny would pack sandwiches and a thermos of tea for her husband and the other workers in the fields threshing hay; the missus had people to make both the hay and the lunch.

The tables would turn when the car parked at the curb of the round church in Ballylanders. Missus would fret with the slip of her dress as she slid behind the organ. Her face might have been deep in concentration but Granny's sweet high singing voice always produced a smile. Missus was now the one looking in awe.

Her voice would join her youngest daughter Anne in song, and that would be the last thing her husband would hear before he died in the room just off the kitchen, right after they choked out a soft rosary between suppressed sobs.

It would not be the first time music brought my grandmother closer to a woman radically different from herself. Her husband not only could fix anything, he would play anything. On any given weekend, he would lash a saxophone to the back of the old bike and pedal into Galbally for the dance. She would see the musical talent all around her and forgo the finer things for herself in an attempt to cultivate that talent with lessons for her four children. Only the son would make a living from music, but all of the offspring would sacrifice money they didn't have throughout their life to encourage the music in each of their children thanks to the example set by their ma.

The finest music teacher in the county was Ms. Steepe, only she wasn't really from around there. She was a Protestant, doing business with my grandmother during a time in rural Fifties Ireland when Catholics were exhorted to go to Confession for entering into a Protestant church.

I sang the melody of "The Lambeth Walk," warm in the notion that my grandmother walked courageous lines in her life for the love of both family and music.

I even "did as I darn well pleasy" and bought the song on i-Tunes, but don't tell the lads from the pub that I'm into show tunes.

Nancy from the North

You could see the look of concern burrowed in my mother's face from a mile away; she had just gotten off the phone with Aunt Nancy in Canada.

"I can't shake the feeling that something is wrong there," she said. "No laughing. She talked slow. It was almost as if she didn't even know who I was."

A call came from my cousin Rob confirming the worst; poor Nancy was in an assisted-living facility under the grip of Alzheimer's.

News like that weighs heavy on my parents, who are in that age group and are in the unenviable position of watching friends and family fall all around them.

Nancy Cleary is one of the more colorful characters in my childhood. Married to my Uncle Paddy on my mom's side, she spoke in a sloppy Dublin slur that could be reined into a melodious brogue when she had to "put on airs."

She ran around the house in curlers most of the time and when she took them out, she would declare that she "could give Joan Collins a run for her money."

She cackled at her own jokes and, unlike my mother, who took out every pot and pan when company came, never cooked (pronounced "kooked" by Aunt Nancy, her lip curling in disgust).

"We don't make dinner around here, luv," she'd say. "We make dinner happen! Sure, I can hardly boil toast!" With that, the room would be filled with that infectious cackle, and even my mother would throw up her hands and join the fits of laughter.

My parents are the practical sort, so we'd make that 12-hour drive up to stay with Nancy and Paddy in Toronto during the years we were saving for the trip to Ireland. At home, we'd only go out to eat if someone died or received a sacrament, or both.

Once we hit Toronto, every meal was either catered in or eaten at a restaurant. "Piece of 'poy,' Paddy?" she'd ask as she fumbled with the box of store-bought apple tart, my baking mother scarcely able to hide her disgust.

Nancy made her living as a demonstrator at the Canadian equivalent of Costco, cheerily placing food samples on toothpicks for the shoppers.

"Sure, any eejit could work the toaster oven," she'd say when I asked her how she cooked things at work but never lifted a pan at home.

Her salesmanship was second to none. When she was hawking asparagus and a shopper explained that he had dentures, she'd coo (in the proper Dublin brogue, not the slang), "Luv, this is so tender yeh can gum it!"

Ever the charmer, she'd gently scold the greedy shopper who had the nerve to come back for a second sample. "Here's my friend again with the gorgeous tie," she'd say loudly, shaming the poor fellow and letting everyone around him know that she was nobody's fool.

There was a deafening silence in the house and the laughter had stopped when I paid my last visit to Toronto. Uncle Paddy was a fraction of his old self, his body ravaged by cancer. His soft blue eyes danced and he wheezed, "There's my Yank Kennobler" as I took his withered frame into my arms for the last time.

Nancy offered to make me a plate of eggs and I looked at her in disbelief. "No more going out for us, luv, it's pots and pans for me now," she said with a sigh as she turned her back to hide the tear that streaked her face. "We stay home a lot now, eh, Paddy?"

News of Nancy's condition is a sobering reminder that a relationship is a fleeting thing, though I don't think I'll ever forget Nancy from the North.

Prom Nightmares

I pulled into our driveway over the weekend and looked over at the lawn next to ours. The toothy teen class president who lives next door was decked out in a tuxedo, posing with his girlfriend as their parents clicked cameras at every angle.

It took me back to my junior prom, possibly the worst night of my life.

The relationship with my girlfriend was winding down—at least that's how it was in my mind. She seemed so excited to go to the prom that she either didn't notice that things were cooling off or she was in denial.

I had already moved on, my eye wandering to an old friend from grade school who had magically developed breasts and curves over the last year. She had a crush on a black guy at school but her Italian parents would have killed her if they knew about it, so she took me to her own prom as a decoy, a few weeks before mine.

Her father stared at me hard. I might not have been black, but I was still in possession of a baby-making pistol under my cummerbund. Her mother was a slow, meandering cow of a woman who obliviously fussed with Sue's soft purple taffeta dress. I couldn't believe my luck that Sue had said yes and was committed to get her mind off the dark side, so to speak.

Taking a cue from the King of Pop, who was riding high on the top of the charts with *Thriller* at the time, I decided to "black up" my outfit with one white glove.

I pulled up to the curb at her house, and the laughs from her brothers began. With my tux, mullet, and pear shape, I looked about as urbane as Pat Boone in a 50 Cent video.

"I knew it was the right call to bring you," she squealed, pointing at the white glove in between fits of laughter. "I knew you'd keep my mind off of Jeremy. You look ridiculous!" I tried not to cry with embarrassment into my one white glove as my stomach somersaulted. Within minutes of our arrival at the prom, she scampered off to Jeremy's table and left me to fend for myself.

I have it on good authority she lost her virginity that night, but I was miles away from her in both heart and mind as she hopped in Jeremy's car for the traditional sleep on the beach that every Jersey kid does after their prom.

I was still hurting from that humiliation as the tailor fussed with my black tux a few weeks later for my own prom. I could see my girlfriend, Linda, standing behind the mirror, beaming.

"You look amazing," she sighed. "I want this kind of tux on you when we get married."

She had it in her head that we were going to get married right after graduation! Hadn't she seen the warning signs that I was no longer interested? Looking back, I was probably to blame. The idea of getting married was one that I neither encouraged or discouraged.

Neither sets of our parents had college educations but they raised their kids with completely different sets of ideals. Her parents were nestled in a leafy neighborhood in Sewaren, living and working in the midst of the nearby oil refineries. Her older brothers and sisters also seemed perfectly content to live at home and work at factory jobs into their twenties.

My parents were committed to having my brother and I land on a higher rung of the socioeconomic ladder than they did, which is why they worked two jobs each and sent us to one of the finest Catholic high schools in the state. They weren't feeding my head with ambition but there was a vague expectation that I wouldn't have a job that required a name tag. I wasn't sure how college was going to work out but I knew that working under a chassis as part of a Jiffy Lube pit crew with a pregnant girlfriend at home was a fate I wanted to avoid.

I could already hear the geyser of guilt that would come from my mother and have made the BP oil spill look tame. "I worked that hard for tuition payments and *this* is what you did with your life?" It was a strong motivator to stay on course for college.

What's more, my mother passionately hated Linda and the nightly "You can do so much better than that" pep talks were starting to take their toll. There were also the comments from a friend of mine ringing in my ears each time Linda and I kissed.

"She's a moped chick," he said flatly.

"What's that?" I asked.

"She's fun to ride until a friend sees you!"

She wasn't great-looking but neither was I, so I was in no position to judge. Few girls were attracted to my Osmond-bastard-child look, so who was I to turn down any attention from the opposite sex? She did have a nice set of legs, which is where I directed my focus. More importantly, Linda could drive a car; she was a year older.

"You really look like hell," my mother said a few days before the prom. "Are you feeling all right? You're all blotchy."

Even though I was feverish and itchy, I shrugged and blamed it on a case of nerves. My mother wasn't buying it, and off to the doctor I went.

"It's chicken pox," he declared. "By the looks of it, you've done your fair share of scratching. You better knock that off or you'll get a face full of scars."

Linda cawed when she got the news. We were in the car.

"Do you know how much my father paid for my dress? You're not backing out of this. I don't care how sick you are!"

"Fine, I'll do it, but then that's the end."

There was a pause.

"End of what?" she asked tentatively.

"Us. I'm just done."

Just thinking about it now as I write this makes me cringe. Of course, there is no good way to break up with someone but you are so ill-equipped in the finer points of diplomacy when you are 16 years old. You have yet to master the "It's not you, it's me" speech—that comes later in college. She screeched the wheels of the car before stopping a few houses away, no doubt melting into tears on the steering wheel.

Came the big night, and my mother tried to hide the angry, scabby red bumps with a mixture of calamine lotion and pancake makeup. She took pictures at a safe distance (no close-ups) and we were on our way.

The rest of the night was a haze of fussing with elastic waist tuxedo pants that cut into the chickenpox bumps along my underwear line, primping feathered hair (mine, not hers), and shuffling around the dance floor as one cheesy Eighties ballad after another played on. I found a box of pictures recently and in them, I look uncomfortable and bored while she looks completely heartbroken.

Back to now. I saw the neighbor the next day and remarked how good her son and his date looked. She rolled her eyes.

"Did you see the skank he brought last night? Chips on the nails, whore's dress and all? I am so glad they broke up last night. They had the most miserable evening you can imagine!"

Lady, you don't know the half of it.

Sending Love with Onion Paper

I got a few big files dropped into my e-mail box over the weekend, pictures of my dad's side of the family celebrating Uncle Paddy's 80th birthday in a fancy restaurant. Everyone is all smiles in most shots, though the spry octogenarian bachelor is cautiously watching over the young ones like a hawk in the photos as they make sugar soup with their ice cream sundaes.

It got me thinking about how we communicated with our family in Ireland over the years. I'm sure this column might date me a bit, but even getting a phone call was a novelty as little as 20 years ago.

I remember well the heart-wrenching good-byes that followed an extensive visit from my grandmother when I was in college. "We'll get you a phone in the house," my mother promised as they brushed back tears at the airport. I don't think any of us imagined the pain and suffering we had just signed up for.

My mother's birthplace is in Ballylanders, a far-flung town in County Limerick near Tipperary that served as a commuting town for workers in the nearby Mitchelstown dairy. The house was a plain cottage along a one-lane road, overgrown greenery clogging the thin strip of blacktop on either side. It took my parents months of overtime pay and waitress tips to afford not only the dial tone in her house but every telephone pole required to extend wires from her cottage to the main road! That seems inconceivable now when you consider that Ireland has surpassed us in mobile phone technology, but that was the state of affairs less than 25 years ago.

Before that, we wrote—on onion paper. Does anyone out there remember that? Onionskin paper was a type of very lightweight, almost translucent parchment which was as thin as the outer skin of an onion.

If you don't have any around the house, break out your Bible and feel the pages—you know, that big book that Catholics let others read to us on Sundays so we can abide by what's in it. Anyway, the onion paper was thin but durable, thanks to the high percentage of cotton fibers woven within.

Onion paper was used because it was so lightweight. When you lived in a working-class household, the price of an air mail stamp was a bit of a luxury and with four people in the house eager to tell Grandma about our Yank lives, you wanted that lone stamp to lift as many pages overseas as possible.

Old habits die hard. I usually send out the photo greeting cards with a holiday note to the Irish relatives each Christmas. "That's gonna cost you an arm and a leg to mail over," my father huffed as he saw the stack of them on the table last December.

Writing letters on onion paper gave me skills that I still use to this day. First and foremost, it gave me valuable experience creating a life far different from my own using cleverly chosen words, something that comes in handy when writing fiction. My letters would be chock full of whoppers about how everything was great, with stellar grades coming home each marking period and girls pounding on the door for dates in between.

The onion paper was too thin to have lines, so you would have to put lined paper underneath it to guide your hand. Eventually, you learned to write straight on your own and my wife still marvels how linear my penmanship is when I scribble some sentiment at the bottom of a greeting card.

It also taught me how to actually put full sentences on a paper, which is a concept that eludes my texting daughters. Things were not "GR8" if you made a spelling mistake and ruined a perfectly good piece of onion paper when you had to start over. Penmanship and grammar had to be perfect, "'Cause why the hell am I shelling out for a good Catholic school education when I could easily save money and ship you to public school?"

The next big wave of communication with the folks in Athenry might very well be Facebook. My cousin's wife just "friended" me and it was delightful to see photos of my apple-cheeked toddling cousins online. "I wouldn't hold my breath on that," Yvonne wrote when I asked her to get the rest of the crew to join our online community. "I'm afraid it's all about the rotary phone with most of the family here in Pollsellagh."

Phones and, of course, onion paper.

A Whiter Shade of Pale

I'm never so grateful for my close proximity to the shoreline as I am on a week like this, when temperatures never dip below the 90s. My wife and I love loading the beach chairs in the car after 3 PM, when the sun relents and the crowds thin out a bit.

On one such night last week, I spotted my younger daughter walking away from the friends who weaved through the crashing waves. Her bottom lip was quivering as she plopped onto the beach chair. "I hate my body," she grunted. Since preteen female self-esteem issues are my wife's concern, I looked over the top of my book at Barbara and nodded my head in my daughter's direction.

"Everything okay, honey?" my wife asked Maura gingerly.

"I hate walking near Olivia on the beach," she cried. "I'm so pale next to her, we look like a black-and-white cookie when we walk together!"

I suppressed a laugh to myself, wondering when I could next weave that killer line into a story (here's that chance!) and tried to empathize with my child. Olivia is an exotically beautiful girl with Portuguese blood that toasts her skin into a dark almond color when exposed to the sun, whereas my daughter is a stereotypical Irish kid with dense patches of freckles on each round cheek.

We live in a part of the Jersey Shore called the Irish Riviera, where the whiteness of the beaches are matched only by the paleness of our skin. We Irish might be known for our wit and intelligence, but we fall short of that tan and trim aesthetic image of summer.

At least *I'm* not trim. I usually park my beach chair as close to the shoreline so that no one sees me topless because I look like uncooked pizza dough that someone used to mop the floor of a barber shop when I take my shirt off. The red berry skin tags that dot my ribcage and the white sunblock crusting around the nipples of my B-cup man-boobs add to the beach blanket fright-fest that is my disrobing. As usual, I deflect the uncomfortable situation with humor, which is why I usually wear a shirt that says either "winning the war against anorexia" or "preparing for famine" that I bought in multiple colors to coordinate with each bathing suit in my wardrobe. Being a plus-sized narrowback might be unattractive, but not being color-coordinated is a crime punishable by death!

The green salt water becomes translucent as the hot sun beats down on it, making my pale belly look like a wonton in broth as I backstroke my way out of a rip current. When the waves overcome me on this day of rough surf, I get batted around by the angry sea before being unceremoniously tossed around with the empty black mussel shells, slithering on the shoreline like the emotionally wounded beluga that I am.

Despite this pasty humiliation, I somehow feel good about giving my kids an ocean full of beach memories from their childhood that I never got. My parents took us to Ireland, where the sun hasn't been seen for a week straight since Haughey was Taoiseach. In the years we didn't go overseas, we parked ourselves by a pool in the Catskills to beat the heat of Jersey City because my parents reasoned that the sun at the beach is more savage than the sun in the mountains.

We now know that the damaging rays of the sun are inescapable, no matter where they beam down on you. Sunscreen technology wasn't what it was back then; we didn't have the benefit of alcohol sprays that dry instantly on your skin. I vaguely remember occasional slatherings of white lotion that would only work if it was allowed to dry into your skin; that time period would be an eternity for a kid itching to go in the pool and I usually dove into the water long before the sunblock would take effect. My folly was rewarded in the evenings with scorched red skin and heat blisters that made my arms and shoulders look like a McDonald's Braille menu. Mom would apply aloe after the fact, sending me to sleep in the throes of alternating shivers and heat flashes.

"You get the skin you deserve," a friend of mine said recently. If that is the case, I am entitled to the best. I now moisturize with a shockingly expensive SPF 30 face lotion and apply a different blocking agent for my scalp. My dermatologist says this 44-year-old face has the skin of a 30-year-old on it, but he wasn't so kind about my skin's condition by the time he got to my underwear line during my last visit. It was there that he gouged away the margins around a few precancerous lesions and stitched the holes left behind.

I sigh and return to my book on the beach, but not before telling my daughter that God never intended the Irish to be tan.

That's just the way the black and white cookie crumbles.

Your Tango

Note: I have been penning some anonymous columns on yourtango.com, a women's online magazine. Yours truly has been writing "the man's perspective" on certain subjects. Now, "deep throat" is revealed in the following three columns:

I Hope My Kids Marry Someone Just Like Me...I Think...

SWF seeks an out-of-shape, weekend-binge-drinking man-child who still goes to Kiss concerts and cannot kick his comic-book habit even though he's well into his forties. Must be choked by the umbilical cord of a domineering mother and live in a state of perpetual Catholic guilt that flares up when he misses Mass on Sunday or lingers too long on a nasty corner of the Web. Lasting three minutes in the sack mandatory; five minutes a plus.

Good God.

My elder daughter, who's 12, is just beginning to show an interest in boys, and since it's every man's dream to have his little princess marry a guy just like her father, I'm trying to craft a personal ad to attract the ideal candidate.

Though my daughter's dating debut is *at least* 10 years down the line, I find that I have a problem: I am horrified by the man I envision her with. Because, in reality, who the heck would date me? Then again, the kid could do worse....

I often wonder what kind of guys are going to come a-calling to our house. While I'm not sure I'd really want a mirror image of myself on the doorstep, I'd like to think that my involvement in my daughters' creation and formation will create loving women who will be able to differentiate between the nice guys and the jerks.

Like most fathers, I have a recurring nightmare that my daughter's prom date will pick her up in a late-model convertible with a Confederate flag painted on the hood, the wind having its way with his mullet as he rounds the corner of our cul-de-sac. He'll ring the bell, offer me some Skoal from a tin that makes a permanent round impression in the back pocket of his powder-blue tuxedo, and reassure me of his love for my child by hiking up his pant leg and showing me a tattoo of my kid's name on his hairy calf.

John Mayer is right about a couple things. One, dating Jennifer Aniston. The other is in "Daughters," when he sings the lines "Fathers be good to your daughters/daughters will love like you do/girls become lovers that turn into mothers."

Long before I first heard that song, I was completely present to the fact that I was going to be the blueprint for every relationship my girls would have with the opposite sex. Parental influences definitely played out when my wife married me, and I studied the parallels between our marriage and the relationship between my wife and her father carefully over the years. Though I was not a brilliant Jewish oncologist who compulsively cheated the house at a poker table in the bowels of Caesar's casino, there were undeniable similarities: our love for puns and storytelling, waking up in Manhattan, reading the Sunday *New York Times*, and an intense devotion to and respect for the woman I married.

I would like to think my girls have learned a lot about relationships from watching me and my wife. They have hopefully seen that being married to your best friend keeps your hair from going prematurely grey, using an "inside voice" at all times gets you a lot further than yelling, and that winning an argument while laying waste to your opponent rarely feels good the next morning.

They've probably figured out by now that if two college sweethearts invest the energy into keeping one another intellectually, emotionally, and sexually stimulated, it is possible to build a nurturing household that will support loving human beings two decades later.

I'm not so vain to think that anyone other than my wife would find my aura hot, but I do know that my daughters could do a lot worse than me in the boyfriend department. And hey, if that boyfriend happens to be a pudgy dude who wears a vintage KISS T-shirt when he picks up my little girl, I will look into the heavens and wink at my Maker.

Take It Off and Lighten Up!

During a recent business trip, I found myself shoe-horned into the back of a taxi with colleagues in various stages of inebriation, hurtling through chancy neighborhoods in Baltimore. I was on my Blackberry with my wife, going through the litany of "kids/mail/bills/when are you coming home/ this single-mother crap is getting old" when the cabbie abruptly stopped at our destination.

"Gotta go, hon," I said. "We just pulled up to the strip club." My colleagues turned their heads my way, mouths open.

"You told her you were going here tonight?" one colleague asked incredulously.

"My wife would throw my shit on the lawn faster than you could say divorce lawyer," slurred the client we'd been wining and dining that evening.

The panicked look on my co-workers' faces said it all: most men are terrified to admit to what really transpires on the road—and what inspires them in the bedroom when they come home.

Let's be clear: if your man plies his trade taking client abuse or has ever attended a conference that finds him in a hotel banquet hall for 12 hours of Powerpoint torture, you can assume your honey has blown off steam, at least once, by contributing to some gal's plastic surgery fund, one crumpled bill at a time.

I am the garden-variety business-traveling strip club patron, for whom a lap dance with a client happens once or twice a decade and is like a harmless game of golf. You tuck a dollar bill or five or 20 inside a G-string, sit back for an innocent bump n' grind, have a few laughs with associates over the thundering drums of a Mötley Crüe song, wonder where your money went as you comb the sticky carpet looking for stray bills around your seat, and leave the joint lighter of both heart and wallet.

My wife knows she has absolutely nothing to worry about, and neither do most women. She knows I would not blow her trust by paying a scantily clad woman $500 to take my pasty, fat married ass into some back room for an hour. No good can come of that. Plus I'm too lazy to bulldoze my tracks and too cheap to burn a good Brooks Brothers shirt when perfume and glitter won't come out of the fabric.

There is also the delicate issue of what I will call "stripper math." When your daughter is a teenager and the girl dancing on the pole is a freshman in college, subtracting their age differences has a funny way of subtracting any sexual stimulation almost immediately!

Now, that's not a wholesale guarantee of good male behavior, and I don't pretend to represent mankind as a whole. My wife and I have been married for 18 years; the drama quotient is remarkably low, the passion remarkably hot and we've never needed any chemical or psychological intermediaries to keep it that way.

"You can take care of yourself to your heart's content in a hotel room, but you best not bring thoughts of that filth into my bedroom," declared one of my wife's friends when I intentionally brought up the subject of shaker bars at our holiday party. Interestingly, she said this to no one in particular at maximum volume, avoiding the gaze of her husband. From my vantage point, it looked like the mini-quiche he was swallowing suddenly turned to broken glass.

I see this as proof that this woman and the other gals who nodded in agreement are in deep denial over what constitutes healthy male sexuality.

Do I bring my stripper-induced sensory overload into the bedroom? You bet I do! My wife and I have known each other since college, and over the years we have achieved the perfect blend of familiarity and mystery by sharing fantasies without breaking trust. Though she doesn't bring a director and makeup trailer to bed, I'm sure that some nights after a *Mad Men* episode I am her John Hamm understudy. Sex is not only about love, but about play as well, and if she closes her eyes once in a while to pretend she is riding someone's see-saw, that's OK by me.

After years of monogamy and two kids, sexuality is not the stuff of romance novels. It's not that easy and never that clean. Some men fish off the company pier. Others, men who are committed to keeping their wedding vow, rely on chemical compounds or are blessed with an on/off switch that allows them to achieve white-hot arousal at the drop of a hat.

Those of us in the middle of the pack build steam throughout the day. Our fire is stoked by a variety of sights and sounds: curves traced in a tight sweater, lingering fantasies of a threesome that includes First Ladies, vice presidential hopefuls, and someone from your wife's Bible study group, and yes, strip club memories.

These are the croutons floating in the sexual stew you get served at night. According to Viagra's website, more than half the men over the age of forty grapple with erectile dysfunction. If enjoying a healthy sex life at that age means getting help from a woman, a pole and pair of ridiculously high Lucite heels, consider yourself lucky. Sexual arousal is a lot like a garment produced in a Kathie Lee Gifford sweatshop: you should enjoy it for what it is instead of obsessing over what went into creating it.

The Irish Curse Is a Blessing

In one of those fluke happy accidents in life, I now count my wife's ex-boyfriend among my closest friends. Phil and I used to eye one another cautiously over the years like the competitors that we were, but that childlike behavior has now eroded as we have both settled into happy marriages with women far above our station.

We have discovered common traits that include a need to constantly poke fun at people around us that eventually gets turned on each other. Sometimes, when the bartender directs pints our way with the speed of an air traffic controller at Newark Liberty during Christmas week, that good-natured ribbing awakens the old rivalry about who might have been better in bed with my missus.

Is there anything more ridiculous than two Irishmen comparing the length of the wand and the magic of the stick with each other, given the bum reputation that our race has in that department? In fact, it is quite acceptable to make fun of the state of our horizontal challenges even on Broadway; Martin Casella has had successful runs on both sides of the Atlantic with his comedic play called *The Irish Curse*.

As a service to you, dear reader, I decided to do some research. The burning question is: what size is normal? The answer is that the unit comes in all shapes and sizes and almost all are "normal," according to the IrishHealth.com. Research from that site shows that the average length of the erect male penis worldwide is just over five inches (12.8 centimeters). The article goes on to say that "Irish men are not regarded as being any more or less well endowed as our European neighbors."

During a summer pool party recently, I overheard my wife's friends discreetly disagree on the subject of Irish size.

"I dated an Irish guy once," explained a rather drunk and loud woman in the circle. "He was funny as hell, had those sexy blue eyes and the Colin Farrell brogue goin' for him, the whole nine yards. But then he took off his pants and it looked like an AA battery sticking out of a Brillo pad."

She looked over her shoulder as the women clucked and cackled around her to see if I was a safe distance away (I wasn't) and in a voice that drunks think is a whisper when it is actually a yell to everyone else, turned to my wife.

"Do you have that problem?"

"No complaints whatsoever," she said with an easy smile. I swallowed on a mouthful of Bud Lite Lime, squinting as hard as I could to block a tear. Even if she didn't mean it, I fell in love with her all over again for defending my honor.

Since five inches is the average, that means half of us will have a longer one than average when erect and half will have ones that are shorter than average. I could say that guys like me get theirs to five inches by folding it in half, but I suspect you'd cut through that line of malarkey without even knowing me. IrishHealth.com encourages us to stop "fretting and put that measuring tape away!"

That doesn't stop the anonymous bloggers on the site from baring their soul of misery anyway.

"I am not very well endowed for a man," writes one. "A woman can get a padded bra, is there anything to boost my crotch and confidence. Please help."

Put a sock in it, dude. Literally. Actually, make it two: one in your mouth to keep you from whining about what God didn't give you and then one behind the zipper to make you look like you have more going on than you do. As I learned in my college marketing classes, packaging goes a helluva long way to sell something even if the product inside is "short" of expectations.

"Mine is tiny altogether," writes another. "This is a very awkward problem because I'm good looking enough and I can get a girl mostly whenever I'm in the mood, but it really affects my confidence because I know I can't go any further with a girl because of how tiny it is. I can't go to my doc as he's male and it would kill me."

I went through a period when I was insecure about mine. It started when I slept over my friend Armando's house in high school and I got a peek at another man's enormous equipment for the first time. I normally change names in my writing to protect the innocent but it should be noted that Armando had no problems whatsoever with me mentioning his name in this piece about his piece when I asked his permission. I mean, can you blame him?

Anyway, he worked at a pool club near his home back in 1983 and knew of a hole in the fence that we could sneak through for some night swimming. We called some girls we were interested in at the time and after liberal dosages of peach schnapps and cheap wine, the suggestion was made to go skinny dipping. In seconds, Armando's swimsuit was a puddle around his ankles and he made his way to the diving board. The bounce of that monstrosity was something I will never forget and I remember feeling horrified and completely emasculated as I watched the tip of his thing pierce the pool's water a full five seconds before his stomach did. I spent the rest of the evening at the edge of the pool and made circles in the water with my feet. Of course, my swim trunks remained on the entire time and my shoulders were slumped as Armando, the girls, and something that resembled the Loch Ness Monster with a back ache splashed carelessly around me for the rest of the evening.

Then there's that whole myth around hand and foot size being commensurate with "other sizes," which had me perplexed. With a size 9.5 shoe and fingers that look like Vienna sausages stitched to a pink pillow of a palm, I thought I was cursed for sure!

I remember starting college the next year and eyeing the communal shower situation with unimaginable dread in the dorm complex. It turns out that the experience of showering with other men proved to be liberating when I discovered that, as the Irish Health study proved, I was in the middle to slightly-upper middle (every centimeter counts) of the pack when I dared take a peek.

I'm not sure if I'm plagued with an Irish curse, but I do know I can brag my way out of any situation with a bit of blarney around my wife's ex—and that is an Irish blessing!

Fighting Irish Meets a Jewish Grandmother

You know when you meet the love of your life. You remember exactly where you were, what you were both wearing, and every other little detail on the spark that ignited your mutual passion.

I was so blinded by love when I met my wife that I never asked if she was Irish. I just assumed that with the reddish hair, pale skin, and freckled face, she was a woman of our tribe. The parents might have not looked very Irish, but I was convinced I was shaking the hand of an Irishwoman when I met her grandmother Molly. She had warm blue eyes, ruddy puffed cheeks, and dyed reddish brown hair that peeked under a scarf.

"And what county of Ireland are you from, luv," I asked, pouring on the charm with a healthy measure of eye contact and a touch of brogue. Her lips contorted in disgust and she recoiled her hand like she had just dipped it into a bag of warm dog turd. She turned to her granddaughter.

"You didn't tell me he was Irish," she screamed, a web of spit gathering at the ends of her mouth as she grabbed her chest for full effect. "Are you trying to kill me?"

She then turned to her son, my future father-in-law. "Richard, you're okay with this?" A gentle and kind giant who was allergic to confrontation of any sort, he shrugged his shoulders limply and looked to the floor. It was then that I noticed the golden Star of David charm on a thin chain that caught in the tufts of his white chest hair.

Jesus, take the wheel! The love of my life was Jewish!

Though we were worlds apart on all matters Irish, her grandmother and I reached instant common ground: we were both reeling in shock.

Like a wounded grizzly, she flailed at anyone who would listen to her. She glared at Barbara again.

"You find Irish guys attractive? Look at him! He has a button nose and a cute face that makes him look like a muppet! You wanna date a man or a muppet?"

I don't remember why I stepped away from the vehicle at that point, as she was clearly cruising for a middle finger right then and there. I guess I was too concerned with how I was going to break the news to my mother to be that concerned about Molly's rage.

The shock of Molly was matched only by the curveball my mom threw at me when I told her what happened that night.

"That's what going to college is all about," she said flatly. "It's like your cousin Robert says: you go to college to broaden your horizons."

I stared for a moment in disbelief.

"You're not upset? She called me a muppet!"

"Well, that's what you get when you don't stick to your own kind," she replied. "I hooked you up with Margaret from church and yeh turned down your nose at her. Serves yeh right to be in a right mess altogether."

How could I forget that date? Margaret was a plain woman with wind tunnel hair that floated above a string of pearls and a body that made Olive Oyl look buxom by comparison. She stuttered slightly and was a ball of nerves; I took her to a dance and she jumped at the slightest touch, like a wounded gazelle in a lion's den. What little spark that formed during the slow dances was instantly extinguished by my mother, who stayed on the sidelines as a chaperone during the Catholic Youth Organization dance.

"Make sure ye leave enough room between yourselves for the Holy Ghost," she had purred in my ear as Journey's "Faithfully" began oozing from the speakers.

"Ma, if you want to find me a girl, get me one that comes without a 'do not resuscitate order,' for God's sake. She was half-dead."

Mom shrugged her shoulders.

"Well, I'm done picking women for yeh," she spat back. "You can date this Barbara to your heart's content, just don't think about marrying or having kids with someone who's not Catholic." There it was. For the second time in twelve hours, a woman had left me speechless.

Molly, or Baba (the Yiddish word for grandmother) as the family called her, launched into the same story every time she saw me. Apparently, she grew up the only Jewish girl in an Irish neighborhood full of mean kids that stoned her on the playground every chance they got. "Two things I can't stand are prejudiced people and Irish," she would say, blissfully unaware of her own ignorance and hypocrisy.

Barbara stood by my side through this family pressure, refusing to leave me home the next time she was invited to Baba's house. It was a quaint but drab ranch in a working-class neighborhood of Woodbridge, New Jersey, with crocheted pillows tossed on a well-worn couch in the living room. The entire house was in bad need of a paint job, a shocking state of affairs considering how well-to-do her son the doctor was. I looked at the frame of one of the doors, which were smudged with pencil marks that looked like they were there since the Seventies.

"They *were* there in the Seventies," Barbara whispered when I pointed them out. "Baba would make us stand at full attention against the door frame and would mark our height and the date with a pencil throughout the years. Every grandchild is on that wall."

Baba wouldn't acknowledge me at this family gathering, turning to Barbara and asking her what "he" would like for dinner. I did what any self-respecting Irishman would do in this circumstance: I bought Notre Dame T-shirts and sweatshirts in every color imaginable. The leprechaun with clenched fist was not just a mascot of a storied sports franchise, it put her whole family on notice that I would fight for my nationalist identity at any cost. They say that which you resist persists, and I was locked in a battle of wills with Molly for many years.

Barbara and I dated throughout college and as soon as I was out of the house and in a decent financial position, I bought an engagement ring. We announced it at a family gathering in my parents' backyard because I knew my mother would not reveal her displeasure in such a public setting. She turned her head as everyone congratulated us and leaned into the shoulder of Father Frank, a cousin by marriage.

"Don't get me wrong, I love Barbara and I think they're well suited," she whispered to the lanky man in black. "It's just that she's Jewish!"

Father Frank nodded knowingly and patted her hand.

"The Blessed Mother was a Jew, Eileen. So, what the hell are you worried about?"

My mother, who more than anything else was visibly relieved to have something to say to the Rosary Society hen club when they raised their eyebrows, wiped away a tear and welcomed Barbara into our family with open arms from that day forward.

Baba was a much tougher customer when told the news. "Half-breeds," she screeched, shaking her head in disgust. "I have had a hard life and I can't believe I endured that just to see the day when my favorite granddaughter would marry an Irishman and give me half-breed grandchildren!"

They say all little girls marry their father in some form and this proved true in the case of Barbara. Richard and I shared an inquisitive streak and a dry wit that we loved to turn on each other. He pushed his mother aside, both physically and emotionally, as he reached for my hand in congratulations.

I was terrified to have my mother and father meet Baba at the engagement party, but they all got along like a house on fire. My parents identified with this no-nonsense woman who told it like it was, saying she reminded them of my Aunt Mary, who was also in the room and gravitated to "a woman after my own heart."

Baba and I looked at each other with a wary eye, though the meeting with my parents helped me win Baba over eventually by showing her that not all Irish people will greet her with rocks in their hands. Emotions between the two of us warmed slightly and we went through great pains to plan a wedding that would not upset her further.

"I am not going into a church to see my granddaughter get married if you-know-who is dying all over the place on the cross," she said. Her voice elevated and cracked like a donkey's bray when she was defiant, which occurred often when we were together.

"Please, let's keep the peace," Richard pleaded as we set out to find a venue. Mom got her hackles up when I told her that we weren't going to be wed in the church and wherever it took place, we would be married under a chuppah.

"No son of mine will get married on the beach like some hippie, so get that out of your mind altogether," she said, reminding me of diocesan tenets that prohibited weddings outside church walls. "You know Father Frank. He doesn't break church rules for anyone, including family. You are still trying getting married in the church, correct?"

"We should have eloped," fumed Barbara. "These people are losing their minds. As if we don't have enough pressure!"

Upon the suggestion of one of my groomsmen, a graduate of Rutgers University, we found and fell in love with Kirkpatrick Chapel, a rustic church nestled in the middle of a leafy acre of New Jersey's premier campus. We went there in the dark after work and drank in the solemnity of silence.

"Not one cross!" I squealed, turning to the curator and with a nod, we booked it.

Perhaps it was the power of my mother's prayer, but Jesus got a front seat at our nuptials by hook or by crook. Because we booked the chapel after dark, we hadn't noticed the 40-foot Jesus walking through the clouds on a stained-glass window.

"I am not walking down the aisle looking at Him!" Baba bellowed in the back of the church.

With the wind flowing through his sandy hair and his robes licking the clouds, he looked more like a Bee Gee emerging from a steam bath. I said a silent prayer to Him.

"Just tell her it's Barry Gibb in a bathrobe and let's move on!"

Richard grabbed his mother by the hand, firmly encouraging her to knock it off through gritted teeth. She held her head high and walked down the aisle, soaking in the attention she had so desperately sought all along.

Tensions eased considerably during the reception. Barbara and I are rabid music fans and we broke the wedding budget for a large funk band. Despite their black faces, the musicians proved adept at playing "Hava

Nagila" and "The Siege of Ennis" back to back. Thank God the wedding photographer had the good sense to capture my mother and Baba on the dance floor, as it became one of the most memorable moments of our wedding.

I either grew on Baba over time or she simply gave up resisting the idea of an Irishman in her family. Either way, she began to share more of herself and I fell in love with her ability to tell stories and laugh at herself. I feel fortunate I got to hear those stories before a freak bout of cancer invaded the roof of this nonsmoker's mouth and robbed her of the ability to speak.

Her emotions ran high as this once independent woman began packing up her belongings to live with her son. I was in the house during the week she gathered her stuff. Despite her weakness, she grabbed my hand with vigor as I moved one of the many boxes. She gestured for me to put the box down and pointed at the door.

I knew I made it into the family when Baba lined me up against the frame of the door and wrote my name and the day's date next to an etch on the door with the rest of the grandchildren. I returned the favor in kind by putting away the Notre Dame shirts and the aggression that went with them.

The Jewish Catskills

A fond childhood memory: the engine of our white boat of a Cadillac coughing and stumbling under the weight of hauling our family of four up the hills of the Catskill Mountains. My brother would look at me with furrowed eyebrow, worried that the car would gasp its dying breath at the peak. We were fidgeting with excitement in the back seat knowing that we were rapidly approaching the blue-collar Irish vacation paradise known as East Durham.

As the car veered to the left, my mother would point her finger to the cluster of green mountains that jutted out of the ground near the passenger side of the car.

"Those are the Jewish Catskills," Mom would announce from the front seat. "We are going to the Irish ones."

As the hills faded from the rear window, I would always wonder what world existed beyond those mountains. There were no Jewish people in my Irish/Polish neighborhood in Jersey City, making their culture an exotic delicacy.

That curiosity would fade once we pulled into the rootsy town of East Durham. Small white cottages lined a lacquered in-ground pool of our modest mountain resort, which provided few creature comforts. Such a vacation operated well below five-star accommodations but provided significantly greater creature comforts than a camping expedition.

We didn't care. It was a paradise far away from the gritty, sweaty streets within our urban Jersey City landscape and we spent hours in carefree swimming and wiffle ball games. We didn't have much in the way of romance in the hills; most of the heavy petting transpired with llamas at the Catskill Game Farm.

At night, we were dragged to the nightclub at Gavin's with our parents for the céilí dances. Paddy Noonan, Richie O'Shea, Pat Roper, and a host of other top-rate entertainers would whip the crowd into a drunken frenzy with frenetic Irish reels and polkas. Of course, this was akin to Chinese water torture to two young boys at the time, our bored eyes rolling around our heads as we overdosed on sugary bar drinks like Shirley Temples and virgin daiquiris.

Fast forward almost 25 years later. I am married to a Jewish girl who has borne me two toddlers. One evening, my wife got off the phone after a chat with her dad. "Ugh, my parents just booked a family reunion in the Catskills!"

My hands trembled with excitement as I packed and loaded the bags. I was finally going to get a peek behind the elusive Borscht Belt curtain that lurked behind those green mountains!

I took the steps two at a time and entered a lobby that time forgot. The rug was a dizzying checker of orange and yellow squares and that led up to dark paneled walls. Wiry gold sculptures hung from the walls and a tired chandelier with missing glass teardrops drooped from the ceiling.

A bored bellhop at the Raleigh Hotel took our luggage on a trolley lined with dirty blonde shag carpeting. A pair of old Jewish women clicked tiles of their mah-jongg game in the corner; they were outfitted in decorated sweatsuits and hissed judgment over their game as we walked by. I found myself missing the ruddy and jolly faces of the front-desk staff at Gavin's!

Another reminder that we were no longer in East Durham came during dinner. The cold purple borscht soup formed a moat around the bleached boiled potato in the middle and a perfectly symmetrical scoop of cold gefilte fish sat atop a bed of wilted lettuce. This led to a stomach-churning feast of pickled herring, poached eggs, and creamed spinach. Not a banger nor mash in sight on the menu!

"I would harvest a kidney for a Guinness, dude," I said to the waiter, who took a $20 tip and produced a six-pack of the black stuff that was brewed when LaGuardia was mayor of Manhattan. I didn't care. I would have drank battery acid if it removed the residue of greasy cold fish from my tongue.

With a flourish, a woman with a heavy Russian accent announced that Louie Goldstein was playing at 8 in the Swizzlestick Lounge. We swizzled our sticks over to the nightclub, a putrid mixture of mirrored tiles and red velveteen wallpaper. The bar area was dotted with a few patrons more intent on the video keno games than the entertainment.

Right before Louie Goldstein's band launched into a merciless loop of vague jazz, the bartender tapped me on the shoulder.

"State laws prevent the kids from being in the bar," he sniffed. "I'm afraid you can't have them here."

It was a blessing in disguise! I peeled away from the in-laws and took the kids to the game room, where the familiar sounds of Ms. Pac-Man gobbling up circles filled the air.

There was a wide variety of activities for each taste, ranging from bingo to ice skating to cosmetic demos and financial planning seminars. Everyone in our party had a great time.

After being hounded non-stop by my 5-year-old, I donned my swim trunks and we made our way to the pool. There was a cheesy Athens theme in the pool room, with alabaster Greek gods peering through the arches like towel boys. I waded into the pool, painfully aware of the warm spots I swam into that were dangerously close to the little kids in the pool. After my tenth shower, I dressed in a suit and we headed to the cavernous dance hall that held the family cocktail party, marking the end of our weekend.

A wannabe big band began to butcher a ballroom standard, and as older couples paired with one another I looked at my daughter, who had wiggled her way up to the stage and was doing her best *Riverdance* impression to the delight of the band. I looked down my leg to find my wee one clinging for dear life to my pants with one hand as she held a Shirley Temple in the other. Her eyes rolled into her head, completing yet another circle of life.

A new breed of happy Catskills memories was hatched in that moment; they looked dramatically different from mine, yet many elements remained the same. Family dinners and carefree fun would be memories held together with syrup from sweet bar drinks between our two generations.

During a sweaty session of bag detail, I was confronted with the only other Irishman in the place. An oil portrait of JFK looked down at me from the top of the elevator shaft, his mouth forever etched with that bemused playboy smirk. Clearly he had an aerial birds-eye view of the open blouses that passed in and out of the elevator.

I wasn't the only Celt enjoying the sights of this Jew-topia. R.I.P, you sly devil.

Lisdoonvarna Is for Lovers!

How's it goin' there everybody/From Cork, New York, Dundalk, Gortahork and Glenamaddy/Here we are in the County Clare/It's a long, long way from here to there/There's the Burren and the Cliffs of Moher/And the Tulla and the Kilfenora/Flutes and fiddles everywhere/If it's music you want, you should go to Clare.

I sang the words to the Christy Moore's "Lisdoonvarna" for more years than I care to count, but I never dreamed I'd get the chance to be in that town to witness the annual matchmaking festival that inspired Moore.

Matchmaking is one of Ireland's oldest traditions and Lisdoonvarna is the epicenter of the activity for most of it during September and early October.

As soon as my dad and I landed at the airport, my aunts and cousins whisked us to Lisdoonvarna "to give the Yank something to write about back home." I couldn't believe my luck!

The name Lisdoonvarna comes from "Lios Duin Bhearna," which means the *lios* or enclosure of the fort in the gap. The town developed into a tourist center as early as the middle of the 18th century when a top Limerick surgeon discovered the beneficial effects of its mineral waters. People traveled from near and far to bathe in and drink waters rich in iron, sulfur and magnesium, relieving symptoms of such diseases as rheumatism and glandular fever.

The town is more known now for curing the fever of loneliness, as thousands of bachelor farmers descend on the town each weekend in the autumn months. Many of the men I witnessed on the streets were bent and stooped with age, with tufts of white hair jutting from their ears.

What makes them so attractive, you ask? Think about it. These old men never found a wife, manning the homestead with Ma while the brothers and sisters emigrated to America. When Ma dies, they are left with millions of euros worth of farming land and no one to cook the dinner. Plus, they are free of sexually transmitted diseases and romantic baggage. They sound so hot now that even I might date one of the auld fellas!

This brings out legions of rabid women of all shapes and sizes to prowl the main street for any man with a still-beating heart and a fat wallet.

The first bar we visited was thick with soccer hooligans and Celtic cougars. My father ushered my aunts and uncle into the quiet dining room while I waded into the action.

A man and his wife were huddled in the corner in front of a drum machine, he with an accordion and she with a violin and a guitar. They rolled through a series of polkas made famous by Bobby Vinton and the show bands that roamed the countryside in the Sixties. Couples goose-stepped around the dance floor in circles as the bachelors shuffled awkwardly from one foot to the other. I felt sorry for one old fella as he tensed up when a woman sidled up next to him. Could this really be his first experience chatting with a woman?

Being on the right side of 45 has its advantages in an environment like this, because I am like Brad Pitt compared to some of the old codgers nursing their pints in the corner. In the few steps it took between the toilet and the bar, I was leered at no less than six times by women with hunger in their eyes. One of them palmed my ass like a ripe grapefruit at an Amish market as I brushed by her. Her face was red and splotchy and framed by a halo of badly dyed black hair. A missing tooth made a visible gap when she let out a loud cackle, elbowing her prim and proper friend perched on the barstool next to her.

The friend was in her forties with a porcelain complexion that sat below a tight bun of red hair and a wispy polka-dot scarf tied around her slender swan neck. I motioned to the bartender and sent a drink in her direction. She smiled and waved, the pained look of loneliness evaporating from her face as I moved toward her.

I began peppering her with some questions about where she was from and where she lived. She played along for a while before clearing her throat.

"Ye ask a lot of questions and I can tell the Irish accent is fake," she said, eyeing me suspiciously. "You wouldn't be some reporter from the States or something like that, would you?"

I nodded.

"Oh, jaysis," she exclaimed. "I want no part of your piece and I'd appreciate you leaving my name out of it."

She turned around on her barstool to address her friend, who was nowhere to be found. I pointed up the stairs and followed her eyes. She looked horrified as her gal pal guided a drunken college boy upstairs, his limp wrist draped around her broad shoulder. The friend's expression was akin to the dog that finally caught the car bumper: after all that chasing, what the heck were you supposed to do with it?

For the month of September, dances like these run from 12 noon each day and carry on into the small hours of the next morning, according to IrishMatchmaker.com.

The multitudes, they flocked and thronged,

To hear the music and the songs,

Motorbikes and Hi-ace vans,

With bottles - barrels - flagons – cans.

Mighty craic. Loads of frolics,

Pioneers and alcoholics!

Ol' Christy hit the nail on the head with that line! The thin strip of town that is Lisdoonvarna has one road, one Internet cafe, a supermarket, and a bar every ten paces. On this crisp September day, strings of plastic flags were draped between poles, the flags tonguing the breeze as it blew by. Below that, caravans selling everything from fish and chips to CDs to fortunes lined the town square.

A hand-painted sign announcing Madame Bridget's trailer intrigued me but my father grabbed my hand as I walked over for a closer look.

"Yeh wouldn't want to be messing with an auld tinker like that," he warned. "They're mad whores altogether."

Undaunted, I parted the moth-eaten curtain and walked up the cluttered steps into her trailer.

She was an old woman with pale green eyes set in a long face that was losing pigmentation. There was a crystal ball on a table cluttered with mugs of tea; she reached for an outlet and plugged the ball into a socket and it swirled in color.

"How much to get my fortune told?" I asked.

"Ten euro," she replied with a sly smile. "'Tis the yank special. But by jaysis, I can read a bit better with the tarot cards, luv, and that's 20 euros."

We settled on 15 and she got to work. She spread the cards across a tablecloth littered with brown bread crumbs and jam stains and encouraged me to pick three. She took my hand before I picked my first one.

"Are you married, luv?"

"I am."

"And you cheat on her, I suppose?"

"No, never."

She shrugged her shoulders.

"That is a right pity. You have a way with words and I just know ye could talk your way out of anything. I can tell ye make your money with words by looking at the hands, yeh see. They're soft and cultured, the mark of a writer."

Was this a good guess or was she looking at me scribbling notes on my bench across the street?

I picked three cards, one of them was a saint and that meant I was going to live a long life free of illness. She pointed to one that had a half-naked goddess dancing with a snake.

"Someone is going to come at yeh with a business proposal that will make you a rich man in the next few years. He will introduce you to a life and you will live out your years in a beautiful and loving relationship."

"My wife will be pleased to hear that," I replied.

She shrugged again.

"'Tis you that brought up a wife, luv, not me."

Shaken by her low opinion of my fidelity and my marriage, I exited the caravan and walked into a gaggle of older women. I tipped my tweed cap and one of them smiled.

"He'd be a right ride," she hissed before the others cackled down the street, tossing back glances to see if I was paying attention.

The Clare breezes carry a wet chill from the Irish Sea. I leaned into the wind and waved it off, thankful for the warm fires of love that waited for me back in America.

Hit-and-Run Blues

You'd know a man like Michael Ward from a mile away. The yellowed shirt that had seen whiter days was tucked underneath a well worn suit. A thatch of wiry white hair sprouted from the top of his head and his ear canals, yet his appearance somehow revealed a certain level of bohemian elegance. He was threadbare, not in an unkempt way, but in a warm and appealing manner akin to the catcher's mitt that has seen its share of fastballs. If you let your mind wander, you might make up a story that this elderly Leitrim bachelor moved to America to escape the harsh Irish economy of the Seventies and got caught between the Ireland that rolled on without him and the adopted city that most of his friends had long since abandoned when things got good again back home.

I have been thinking about—scratch that, *haunted by*—the news of Michael Ward's death. He was mowed down by a hit-and-run driver on the corner of 1st Avenue and 84th Street last Friday, left to die on a grimy Manhattan curb by someone apparently too impatient to wait for an 85-year-old man to cross the street. I can't get the image out of my head of this kind soul, a man with such a zest for life, convulsing and bleeding on the pavement.

I met Mike only once, at my uncle Bobby Cleary's funeral last December. With Bob plucking the strings of a banjo and Mike hunched over the squeezebox in the pubs around Bainbridge Avenue, the pair had formed a musical conversation in a group called The Limerick Weavers and created a deep friendship that lasted through the decades in the process. They must have delighted thousands of lonesome Irish with songs over the years and would go on to book regular gigs at places like Gorman's, The Bainbridge Cafe, Ireland's 32, and Fiona's. I pray some of those fans remember Mike in their prayers as a way of saying thanks for providing a slice of home when they needed it most.

When a man of his age lugs a heavy accordion over his shoulder and crosses three state lines to pay a musical tribute to a friend, you don't need to know much more about the measures of his loyalty and love that are woven into the fabric of his character.

"Good on yeh, girl," Mike would grunt as Dawn Mulvihill, Bobby's devoted partner of 22 years, played heartbreaking airs on the violin near his coffin. Dawn took the place of Bobby as Mike's sparring partner during the luncheon that followed my uncle's burial and I marveled at how this wee colorful character single-handedly lifted the heavy burden of grief from our family's shoulders. Inspired by his effervescent spirit, many of us took turns on the microphone or the guitar to participate in the joyous musical repartee that brought Mike and Bobby together in the first place.

"I play the accordion for the old folks in the homes now," he said, completely oblivious to the fact that he might have been a good deal older than many of the blue-haired residents in those audiences. He had no sense of his own mortality at all when he strapped on the accordion, melting the years from his small frame. When I mentioned I would be writing about this day in my *Irish Voice* column, he beamed.

"Yerra, someone had to die for me to get my name in lights, and sure, that's the sad state of affairs for yeh." With that said, he threw back his head and let out a tight laugh, but not before reminding me that his name was spelled with no "E" at the end of it.

You want to believe that the hit-and-run driver kept going because he or she may not have even known they hit something. It might have been a pothole that made that loud thump and in this frantic time we live in, the driver's eyes might have been on some mobile device instead of on the road where they belonged. You don't want to believe that the person behind the wheel of the gold Nissan Maxima decided to carry on that night, discarding this kind soul onto the sidewalk like an empty soda bottle. I didn't know the man well, but I know he deserved a more dignified end to his life than what was doled out.

I'm told this eccentric character was a doorman for decades and I can't think of a better person to greet you when you got home after a long day at the office. He no doubt would delight the residents of the building he guarded with a song from his encyclopedic knowledge of Irish music or a story about the auld sod.

You could say that we live in a cruel world that tosses an old man to the side without any regard for the dignity of human life, but I prefer to think that St. Peter had a sudden opening for a doorman at the pearly gates and knew just the man for the job.

Rest in peace, Mike, and tell Bob his nephew misses him deeply.

Right to Choose

The air was thick with the scents of cotton candy and horseshit as I paced around the confines of the rickety wooden stall. The Middlesex County Fair was in full swing, with prize pigs waddling through the crowd on their way to the judging pens. The sounds of an organ grinder met the squeals of children as the rides catapulted them into the humid night.

The year was 1984 and I don't remember the circumstances that found me working the New Jersey Right to Life booth on behalf of our church; it probably had something to do with me having to atone for the sin of spewing vomit on my comforter after a drinking binge.

To my left was one of the newer nuns who had transferred to my parish's grammar school and to my right was Mr. Daly, a man fiercely dedicated to the cause of saving an unborn life. The whiteness of his hair was matched only by the paleness of his skin, which made his determined blue eyes more urgent. He had been arrested many times over the years, pulling stunts like chaining himself to the fence of a Planned Parenthood clinic in protest. I admired the man for his conviction, which made me feel more out of place than I already was.

Growing up, I never could imagine a circumstance where someone would knowingly terminate a pregnancy. That all changed when I hit college and had a few "birth control malfunctions" myself because the condom didn't come with instructions and there was no way I could ask my father how to work one of those things.

"I wouldn't do the crime unless I was prepared to do the time," he might reply over his paper.

Thank God for answering the mega-prayers that finally brought on the late period; I would be lying if the thought of an abortion didn't cross my mind at some level during the agonizing waiting game.

"I didn't ask you how you think about it, I need the help and you're going," my mom exclaimed. "Sure, I'm not breaking my back waiting tables and shouldering the burden of a college education for you to be questioning your faith!"

It was too late for that. Mass attendance was one of the many things about living at home that went by the wayside in dormitory life, along with square meals and clean laundry. An atheist English professor would debate me on my beliefs in organized religion and he was starting to wear me down. I was thinking about his last lecture as I mindlessly passed out pamphlets with pictures of aborted fetuses that looked so much like veal parmigiana that I can't stand to eat it to this day, and then I felt a slap on my wrist that sent the pamphlets flying.

"I want to know what right you have to tell me what to do with my body," screeched a very large woman. Her round, pimply face was framed by curly hair tortured over the years by treatments that come out of a box from the pharmacy. She wore a tie-dyed tank-top dress that swept the dirty fairgrounds as she waddled away from me.

"That's all right, Mike," Mr. Daly said in a reassuring tone. "People like that cannot keep us from getting our message out."

I bent down to pick up the pamphlets and found her face within inches of mine when I stood up.

"I mean, who do you think you are, anyway! It's my body!"

"It's actually God's body," I stammered. "He's just loaning it out to you, ma'am. I'm not sure he made you so that you could go around killing unborn children."

From the corner of my eye, I could see Mr. Daly nodding proudly.

"I'm just thankful for Michael Dukakis and the Democratic Party, who are fighting hard to keep those laws off my body!" she screeched.

"Well, all I can say is that when yourself and Michael Dukakis meet your maker, you'll probably be in the same boat."

"Yesss," whispered the nun behind me. I had an audience now as people gathered around us to see what the fuss was all about.

"Fuck you," roared the woman, enjoying the attention as she brushed the limp hair from her face. "You're probably aren't man enough to knock someone up. That's why you're in here with the rest of these losers."

"Whooooa!" came the collective gasp from the crowd as all eyes turned toward me.

I'm not particularly proud of this, but I do some of my best work in these situations. Being Irish, I must have the last word and love a good fight, and such a victory is almost always achieved at the expense of common sense and decency.

"I'm not sure why you're getting so worked up about this whole abortion thing," I shouted. "I mean, who'd fuck you with your lousy attitude? Shouldn't you be hanging around the pen with the rest of the prize pigs?"

Some tattooed biker high-fived me and as I reached for his palm, my eyes met the horrified gaze of Mr. Daly and the nun in the RTL booth.

"I'm sorry, I'm just not cut out for this," I said as I untied the strings of my apron. "I think this cause deserves more than what I could give it."

News of what I had done would have reached my mother before I got home and I was sure to be greeted with some diatribe about how she couldn't show her face in the church after my stunt. There would be a time and a place to deal with that. At that moment, I just took in a big gulp of night air. Who knew victory smelled like cotton candy and horseshit?

Lemonade and Gas

A roadside lemonade stand is highway robbery, but I always pay it anyway. Who in their right mind would pay 50 cents for a little Dixie cup full of ice and watered down sugar water when a Big Gulp at a 7-Eleven gives you 10 times that amount for a similar price?

Of course, we do it because we want to encourage the little entrepreneurs. In this day and age, when kids assume that money comes out of ATMs, it is heartening to see that some wee ones still know the value of a dollar and how to earn it.

Lemonade stands remind me of my first taste of business during a tumultuous time in our nation's history. I was in seventh grade in 1979, the year that we were in the grips of an energy crisis caused in part by unrest from the Iranian revolution. The price of gas was sky-high and supply was so tight that you were only able to get gas on certain days if your license plate ended with an odd number, and other such contrivances. The summer was steamy, which further cooked the tempers on those long lines.

We had just moved out of Jersey City and into the suburbs that year. I didn't have any friends, so I decided to take over not one but two paper routes to fill the boredom. Making money was an unexpected benefit and when the tips started rolling in, I suddenly developed a fierce mercenary streak that is still part of my genetic makeup today.

Newspapers were dropped off at your house in bundles, with more papers delivered than needed to accommodate for any damages in transit. With two paper routes, I would sometimes get dozens of extra papers.

I was riding home from the paper route with the excess papers weighing me down in a canvas bag with The Home News logo that was slung over my shoulder. One of the drivers on the gas line honked the horn and motioned me over to buy a paper. A chorus of car honks followed and within minutes, I sold all of the papers.

The Home News only charged me for the number of subscribers on my route, so the excess papers that they shipped came at no charge. The 25-cent list price was pure profit whenever I sold them on the gas lines!

I made sure I rode by the gas station every day and I never left the line without completely selling out my supply of papers. I got another newspaper canvas bag, filled it with cans of soda, and slung it over the other shoulder. I sold the paper and a can of soda for a dollar and never rode the bike home with any cans or papers in my bag.

"You know, kid, I'm getting fucked as it is by this goddamn gas station; you're adding insult to injury," cried one driver as he forked over a dollar.

"I like this kid," shouted one driver at the other. He was perched on the hood of his parked car on the long line. "He understands the laws of supply and demand and the little bastard probably didn't even make it out of grammar school yet. He'll go far."

I made no less than $5 per day for less than 10 minutes of work that entire summer. I remember the red 10-speed bike that I had my eye on; it had a hard plastic bulb covering the crossbar to simulate the look of a motorcycle. Within weeks, I had enough money to buy it without any assistance from my parents.

The Iranians eventually stopped fighting with America and one another, bringing an end to the rationing of gas and those long lines. The papers that were worth their weight in gold a week ago were now worthless and I joined my friends at the gas station in mourning the loss of long car lines.

Though I couldn't articulate it at the time, the whole affair taught me the same valuable lessons about pricing against demand and customer service that the kid on the corner with the lemonade stand is now starting to realize.

An Open Letter to Chris Kelly (and Every Other Groom Caught Between an Irish Bride and an Irish Mother)

Hey, Chris:

Well, congratulations on nabbing yourself the genuine article! By placing a ring on my cousin Sinead's finger, you fulfilled a dream no doubt held by every Irish mother to include yours: that you stick with your own kind.

With her name, red hair, milky smooth complexion, warm blue eyes, and the brogue that creeps on you when she is angry or drunk, you could not have proposed to a more Irish bride.

Truth be told, we're damned glad and more than a bit lucky that you are joining the family. Over the last two decades, myself and the cousins have come home with Italians, people "a darker shade than ourselves," same-sex partners, Jews, and other forms of human beings that tested the boundaries of tolerance in our parents. I am happy to say that older generation passed the test beautifully, yet I think they were breathing a sigh of relief that the tests ended when you first walked in the door. "He's one of our own, like," was whispered under their breath.

Now that you are part of the family, allow me to tell you what I think about how you're running your life. This family is good at this and rest assured, I have learned from the best. Get used to it and your life will go smoothly.

My heart really went out to you the other night, as you cradled your big

LCD screen of a head in your hands and massaged your temples as Sinead reeled off one problem after another in the planning of your wedding. Like an LCD, your anguished expression was brought to us in high definition, the beads of sweat dripping furtively from your brow.

Bridesmaids playing chess with offspring! Family members off their meds! Dueling views of what the engagement party and shower should look like! These are all things that could drive a lesser man to drink. You're hanging tough, friend. I like that in a dude.

From my vantage point, it would appear that an epic battle of wills was touched off between your Irish fiancé and your Irish American mother and you are feeling the squeeze. You are looking for a win-win here and I am sorry to tell you that there isn't one.

"I just want to keep the peace," you shouted in an agony that gave Jesus in the garden a run for his money. Like him, you were sweating blood, which was an impressive trick indeed. But Jesus taught us that even that will not keep this cup from passing over you.

In a more heated and inspiring moment, you claimed yourself free of your mother's grip with a defiant "to hell with her and what she thinks." Again, you're fooling yourself if you think this scenario will produce a win.

How do I know all of this? I have experience in these matters, only the cross-fire I found myself in was between my Irish mother, my Jewish wife, and her family. Yeah, I know that it's not exactly the same scenario but it is pretty close: Jewish mothers give Irish mothers a smackdown competition in the guilt department and I will leave it at that.

After the initial shock of proposing to a Jew wore off, my mother seemed hell-bent on making our wedding as Irish as possible in an attempt to distract her friends and neighbors that a rabbi was co-celebrating with our cousin Father Frank on the altar.

Everything was a battle. Mom wanted an Irish band to guide a cast of thousands through "The Siege of Ennis" and "The Chicken Dance." After much protest, we booked a funk band adept at playing both Irish reels and "Hava Nagila."

My bride, Barbara, had picked out a beautiful cake design complete with flowers that were in line with her French country aesthetic. My mother had bought a green and white ceramic cake topper in the shape of a claddagh ring that was engraved with our names and wedding date in gold paint. It was imported from Ireland at great expense and was a grand and sweet gesture, but the effect of putting this on the cake was akin to putting a thatched roof atop the Musee Du Louvre.

"Do you know what I had to do to get that made?" my mother hissed when I told her there was no way that was making it anywhere near the cake. There was no compromise on the morning of the wedding, so my mother essentially placed the cake topper atop the pastry when no one was looking.

That's the kind of scenario that would play out numerous times during our marriage, which has lasted nearly 18 years as of this writing. That's another lesson I've learned: how goeth this wedding will goeth your life. The clashes between mother and wife may be minor in comparison to the ones you are dealing with now because wedding drama is fueling the fire, but the same battle of wills always has you in the middle.

In one corner is a wife that tells you in no uncertain terms to grow a set of balls and stand up to your mother for once in your life. In the other corner, there is a mother who is completely panicked that her little boy no longer leans on her as the axis in which his world turns and will play every trick in the book to have you fly in her orbit. Sound familiar? Thought so.

Consider this letter an early wedding present, for the next sentence contains the secret that unlocks an easy life.

The wrong Missus Kelly is worrying about this.

Feel free to use this when Sinead weighs in on how your mother mollycoddles your sister or complains about perceived slights against you in your role as prodigal son. This sentence also comes in handy when your mother comments about the tone of voice Sinead uses when talking to you, why you are spending so much time with that side of the family instead of your own, how she is feeding you too much or too little, and above all, how your wife cares for the grandchildren should God bless you with them.

Make sure you deliver the senses without a hint of anger, drama, or emotion. Chances are you will have to use this sentence when one of them is emotional and your lack of response will probably drive them nuts!

Saying "the wrong Missus Kelly is worrying about this" often enough will result in both sides getting the hint that you will not tolerate your wife making your mother wrong and vice versa. I know that sounds impossible, given the smog of anguish you are choking on, but a steady diet of *Animal Planet* has taught me that even the most rabid creature can be tamed. This sentence is the chair and whip you will need to keep the tigresses behaving in their respective corners.

Kenny Rogers, as usual, holds the keys to life in one of his songs. Remember the words of "Coward of the County"? It goes like this: *Promise me son/Not to do the things I've done/Walk away from trouble if you can/It won't mean you're weak if you turn the other cheek/I hope, you're old enough to understand/Son, you don't have to fight to be a man.*

That Kenny Rogers is a prophet. He's telling you that when you learn to politely tell your wife or mother that the wrong Mrs. Kelly is worrying about the matter at hand, you learn to scream without raising your voice and reclaim your manhood in the process.

You have an embarrassment of riches on your hands: two good, caring women who are deeply committed to your happiness and greatness. By implementing a little psychology, you can take advantage of both perspectives. They are smart ladies who both have impeccable taste if they love you.

One more thing. I'd like to be seated close to the bar and given the choice of chicken marsala or stuffed salmon, I will pick the fish over fowl.

Mazel tov (Gaelic for good luck),
Mike

Hopelessly Devoted to You, Olivia Newton-John

Are you turned on by women hurtling small appliances at your head in a fit of passion? If you answered yes, click somewhere else, because this mama is not into the drama. SWF, 44, likes her men as she likes her wine: smooth, complex, dark, and flowing with a robust red passion. I can see the inner beauty in any man but you must either be in possession of your own teeth or a reasonable facsimile. If you have a Members Only jacket or a pair of parachute pants in your closet, click somewhere else.

Long walks on the beach are nice but if it's all the same to you, I'd rather sit on the couch with a Domino's pizza box balanced on my knees while you crack open a can of Mountain Dew.

Another day, another friend contacts me and asks me to write her online dating profile. She said she wanted a man more in line with NASCAR than Neiman Marcus and within weeks of posting this, she brought around a series of hulking teddy bears (*ones with tattoos and a trucker caps, but still!*). Though some Manhattan-based matchmakers charge hundreds for the service, I ask for two bottles of good red wine: one for the creative process and one for my personal stash.

I started doing this online profile service as a favor to friends about four years ago. My wine cellar now grows like the ass of a newlywed bride who no longer needs to worry about a dress fitting and I am more effective than roofies in cosmopolitans in causing spontaneous hookups.

Though I am unbelievably fortunate to have married a redhead far above my station, there is a part of me that is deeply resentful in this day and age that my God-given writing talent is a potent tool to attract the opposite sex. We now live in a world of instant messaging, texts, social networks, and a plethora of other mating tools that all rely on clever use of the English language for a special mojo.

Though I am quite sure I could never find anyone that comes close to the caliber of my wife, I fantasize all the time what my dating life would look like if I were unattached right now and using the power of the written word for devious and sexual purposes.

"You're living vicariously through them, I know it," my wife says demurely when she catches me asking our friends for every lurid detail of a date caused by my profile. "Here's another guy who has fallen in love with you," is the subject of an e-mail from my friend Dawn as she forwards dozens of replies from men who have gotten stuck in a web of lies I have spun for her.

When I was dating, the ability to string sentences together was not exactly an aphrodisiac to the girls I pursued. For that, I can only blame Olivia Newton-John.

Allow me to explain. I came of age around 1977, just as Olivia was about to rule the universe. She had just launched a Fifties bobby-sox revival with her big screen reworking of *Grease*; I was pretty good at impressing the seventh-grade girls with my rendition of "The Hand Jive," a whimsical dance from the movie that required flexible wrists and fingers. Just as I was hitting my hand-jive stride, the glorious bitch threw me a curveball a year later with a film called *Xanadu* that cast her as the goddess that she was. The story required the glossy Aussie to glide on a pair of roller skates, igniting a rolling craze that coincided with my first signs of puberty.

For people of a certain age, the roller rink was the place to hang out when you were a teenager, especially when you ran out of quarters to play Asteroids or Space Invaders at the local arcade.

The same place that hosted our ice hockey practices in South Amboy in the early morning hours would be transformed into a sleek roller disco by night. The scene was like a school dance, only with wheels and the constant threat of a broken bone or twisted ligament looming above the dry-ice smoke.

The suggestive lyrics of Donna Summer might have flown above our heads but the propulsive disco beats hit us squarely in our preteen crotches as we rolled around in a giant circle. When the tempo slowed, the boys and girls would skate over to their respective corners. The lineup to choose from all had the same look on the female side: soft cashmere v-neck sweaters and puffy shoulder pad added to the cottony allure of glossy lipstick and feathered hair sculpted in Olivia's image. Some of the boys would burn off testosterone with slick skates and figure-eights in the middle of the circle, where they would show off brawny moves cultivated during the hockey practices that morning. The jocks naturally had the first pick of the litter before the rest of us swooped in for the spoils.

I tried to compensate for my lack of swagger by wearing the latest styles. Robin Williams was flying high at the time with *Mork & Mindy*, so I saved enough paper-route money to buy the rainbow suspenders he made famous on the show. They held up a generously sized pair of parachute pants, a tight-fitting article of clothing made with the same fabric as a real parachute. I remember them making a swishing noise whenever you made the move of putting one foot in front of the other as you skated around the rink. The pants came in the Day-Glo colors that were fashionable at the time; I believe I wore a pair of bright cherry red trousers to match the suspenders.

"You look like a pair of right feckin' eejits altogether," my dad said with a scowl as he dropped my friend and me at the rink. "You'll get your arses kicked in there for wearing that nonsense, you mark my words!"

He was only half right. We did look like eejits but we didn't bring any trouble on ourselves for dressing that way because everyone wore the same thing and looked equally ridiculous.

I would skate by the line and ask one of the girls to join me for a roll on the floor (mind out of the gutter, people). The response was always the same: a grimace of pain followed by a polite "no thanks" that was followed by cackles from the gaggle of friends around her. It was if the girl was mortified that she was giving out the impression that some Casper the Friendly Ghost in parachute pants had a chance with a girl like her. I would skate around the floor, dejected and emasculated, while couples paired off into the dark recesses of the hall.

I do remember one time when I was rewarded by a roll and a kiss. I couldn't believe my luck when it was suggested that we move to a corner for alone time. We were skating off of the main rink and holding hands when I spilled head first over a discarded soda can. A crowd of pointing and laughing skaters gathered around to watch the spectacle of me getting up and the only thing that got stiff that night was my sprained ankle.

I sometimes wonder how things would have been different if only Olivia had made a movie about the life of James Joyce in the Seventies. In this version of Bloomsday, she would have played a hot-and-bothered Nora Barnacle who could scarcely contain herself around the literary sexiness of a Dublin scribe. Having a sex symbol of that caliber whisper "Let's get physical" into the ear of an Irish writer would have made the whole dating thing a hell of a lot easier for a shy, insecure kid with a love for words.

Instead, I am reduced to a Cyrano de Bergerac for the cyber-age, helping others say "I honestly love you" to their soul mate with a well constructed online profile.

Let's Not Focus on That ..

My 9-year-old daughter hopped into the car after a particularly strenuous afternoon of ballet not long ago and as the car door shut, I asked her how practice went.

"It was okay," she replied, shrugging her shoulders. "Mr. Dan was in a good mood, so that made practice fun. But Caitlin called me fat today, which kinda hurt my feelings."

"How did that make you feel?"

"Just great!" she said sarcastically, rolling her eyes.

"What did you say to her?"

"I said, 'let's not focus on that, okay?' Then she dropped it."

I was stunned at the poise, grace, and self-assurance she displayed in the face of a cruel schoolyard dig that would have brought both of her parents to their knees back in the day. Both my wife and I have struggled with weight issues in the past and comments from a ballet bully bring us right back to that time in our lives when we were teased by the other kids for being plump.

I had a similar experience to hers that did not go nearly as well. I remember being about my daughter's age and belonging to a Boy Scout troop in Jersey City. The scout master was choreographing this elaborate Indian dance in the church basement one Tuesday evening. We had been practicing for weeks, interweaving hula hoops to create the illusion of wings as we hopped around to the beat of tribal drumming. The scoutmaster had ordered our costumes, which consisted of shorts, a black braided wig, and a sash depicting cave drawings that was slung over one shoulder. I swallowed hard when he unpacked and handed out the costumes.

"Where are the shirts?" I asked.

"There are no shirts," he replied. "These are Indians. No one wore shirts."

This was a problem. I had a layer of pale, cratered flesh that hung over my belt like a volcano of cottage cheese and an ample cleavage swung above the whole mess at my waist. I was terribly self conscious of my body and with good reason. When I took off my shirt, the boys started to laugh. Even my best friend at the time turned on me.

"Look at those boobies," Billy squealed.

"Look how skinny you are," I shot back. "You look like a French fry dipped in ketchup with that red hair."

At that moment, the heat was deflected off me and before long, the lads in the troop began making fun of one another's body.

This bought me just enough time to approach the scoutmaster with an idea.

"Since I am shadowing Billy in these dances, wouldn't it be cool if I looked like a shadow?" On the day of the show, I stepped onto the stage wearing a black leotard and dark face paint. The color was not only slimming, it cloaked a poor self-image that has plagued me ever since.

It also produced a pattern of behavior that served me well over the years: when things get hot and someone is picking on you, give it right back to them with a dollop of cutting Irish humor that cripples your opponent.

I remember a rough first week at a new grammar school into which my brother Brendan and I transferred after my parents moved us into suburban Central Jersey. I was in seventh grade at the time and Brendan was a fourth-grader with a cast around his abdomen to correct scoliosis, an abnormal curvature of his spine.

We were getting changed in the boys' locker room and one of the big kids decided to test the new boys in town. As Brendan was taking off his shirt, he was shoved onto the ground and struggled to get up because of the limited movement the cast provided.

"He's like a turtle!" a fat kid who was stripped down to his underwear exclaimed before jiggling into convulsive laughter.

"Your tits are bigger than my mother's," I yelled. "You have nothing to laugh at."

The bully turned his attention on the fat kid and I had just enough time to help Brendan off the floor and out of the room.

The witty comebacks displayed an external confidence that was a far cry from my true inner workings. I can still feel the pain of standing in the middle of the Sears boys section with my mother and brother. Brendan was slim and wiry, the ideal body type the designers had in mind when they put together their clothes. I would look longingly at the countless shirts and tops he so effortlessly mixed and matched while mom would look through the racks and hum contentedly.

The music would stop when it was my turn to shop. For both mother and child, this experience was as messy and painful as childbirth itself. I would be dragged, against my will, to the "husky" section of the store. In this section hung a putrid, measly selection of checkered Toughskin pants that made me wonder if Sears was joining in the chorus of fat kids' mockery by designing unflattering patterns to go on my big ass. The Toughskin material was only slightly smoother than burlap because, well, it had to be.

"Sure, your father and I are not made of money, you know," my mom replied when I asked her why I had to wear the Toughskins. "These pants have to last until Easter, and then we'll be back. God knows what size ye'll be by then."

As my daughter edges toward puberty, she has begun to show signs of loathing her body. She has taken this head-on, asking for help to take control of her shape and we have employed a personal trainer to help the entire family support her weight loss through exercise and good eating.

She is obsessed with the Food Network and goes to great pains to develop lowfat versions of the dishes they make on those shows.

I never developed a healthy relationship with food and exercise and certainly never had the class or confidence in myself to politely advise an opponent to drop the conversation about size the way my daughter does. She goes through life carrying her weight with supersized style to the point that, well, you really don't focus on her weight. She is my inspiration.

I grew up to be pleasantly plump and I love to eat, yet I strive to attain my daughter's mastery of bullies to this day.

Case in point. I drove by my old central Jersey neighborhood this week, stopped at my favorite sub shop and was greeted at the counter by Danny, the bully who pushed my brother down all those years ago.

He had a mangy beard, ripped jeans and a leather biker's vest over a Harley t-shirt that told me all I needed to know about how he was unable to break the tangle of our town's blue collar roots.

There wasn't an ounce of Catholic compassion in me as I told him in painstaking detail how thin I wanted the Swiss cheese cut for my sandwich. I threw a dollar into the tip jar in the counter, but the encounter was priceless.

Am I immature?

Uh-huh.

Do old bully wounds still fester, 33 years later?

Yup.

Does the daughter have a lot more grace than the dad in these circumstances?

Well, I suppose I can't slice that reality thin enough to make it easier to swallow.

Have a Heart!

You can tell my father was a farmer in Athenry by the way he attacks my property. With a pick and shovel, he tore at the roots of a cranky stump one afternoon, a skill no doubt honed from digging for spuds in his youth. We were preparing the yard for an onslaught of toddlers in my house who were itching to get out and play in the yard after a cold, punishing winter.

The previous owners of this house I just bought had built a sand pit underneath an expensive swing set. Unfortunately, it moved along with them as part of our deal and I was stuck with a space overrun with weeds that popped up from the tired and thin layer of sand in the pit. While dad worked on raking the flower beds on this cold spring morning, I prepared the pit for an imminent truckload of sand that would be dumped into the space.

"Every feckin' cat in the neighborhood will be using this to wipe its arse," Dad grunted, shaking his head at my stupidity. He had a point. From that day forward, I spent each morning combing the sand for cat waste before plopping the kids into their play space.

One morning, I noticed a gaping hole in one of the corners. I bent down to investigate what I thought was a sinkhole in the sand and got the shock of my life when a large gopher scurried between my legs and into his new home.

Because I am essentially useless around the house, I called my father.

"I'll be right down," he said flatly. Within the hour, he came with a Havahart trap under his arm. A rectangular box made of wire with an opening on one end, the doorway would snap shut when a lever inside the cage was triggered by the rodent's paw.

We set the trap with green goodies near the hole and the next morning, I was awoken by the sounds of a fat gopher clawing at the confines at the cage.

I went to call Dad again but saw his car in the driveway already. He picked up the trap, which wobbled as the animal wriggled inside.

"Where are you going with him?"

"Not your concern," he said and off he went. I'm not sure if he let the animal off a few miles down the road or if he brought it to his Cork neighbor for target practice. As the man said, it's just not my concern.

The gopher had friends in the den, and we emptied the cage four more times. On the fifth day, I went out into the yard and looked a different species in the eye. It looked like a giant rat, with cold black eyes at the top of a pointy white mask of face. He sat in the cage, a long white tail tucked underneath a thatch of grey fur.

"What in Christ's name is that?" Dad asked over my shoulder. He took another step and the animal let out an ungodly howl and revealed a mouth full of razor sharp teeth.

"By Jesus, a fellow like that would turn right on you if you let it out of the cage," Dad reasoned. "This fecker has got to go."

Ignoring the design and intent of the "have a heart" trap, Dad produced a broom from the shed and removed the bristles before jamming the handle through the wire. He jabbed the animal repeatedly until it assumed a fetal position and stopped breathing.

We approached the cage again; we were inches away when the animal sprang to life and snarled at us.

"Well, we just got our answer on what it is," I said. "He just 'played possum' or played dead."

"Well, he snarls at me like that and that fecker isn't coming out alive," my dad said with a grunt before lunging at the cage again.

"This. Is. The. Hardest. Animal. I've. Had. To. Kill," grunted Dad in between jabs at the possum.

"How many more victims have you had?"

"Use your feckin' head, yeh eejit! I was raised on a farm!"

I decided to stop the madness and lugged a large garbage can over to the side of the house, away from the view of any neighbors. I filled it with water and in an act of mercy, brought the cage over to the can and dropped it in. The defiant animal clawed at the side of the cage for one more breath before being fully submerged into the water.

"There's still bubbles coming out of that thing!" exclaimed Dad. "Can yeh believe that?"

With one last gasp, the animal died on the grates of the trap that had no heart. In a battle of wills between possum and a grandfather hell-bent on protecting his grandchildren, 2 legs are better than four.

The Drunk Clown

I'm reading this book called *Pathways to Greatness* by Scott Asalone and Jan Sparrow. Culled from hundreds of surveys, the book makes conclusions about what makes people great. In an essay titled "Inquire Within," the authors encourage everyone to "stake out time for personal introspection and ask who am I? What do I want to be? What do I believe?"

I know that now, but I didn't know it back in 1995. I was out of school seven years, amassing a reputation in my company as a high-octane salesperson who never met a quota he didn't hit.

I was in a competitive laboratory-supply distribution business and ran with a crowd of hard workers and hard drinkers. One after one, my mates fell around me, attending church basement meetings to atone for sins against the liver, tamed into domesticity by a worried wife at home, or going over to the dark side of management. No problem—more booze for me!

"Is that all you're going to be: a sales rep?" asked my mom one day over Christmas dinner before launching into descriptions of cousin Rob's big vice-presidential job at a bank or how one of the Gallagher kids had been rising up the ranks at CBS. Though I was an adult with a wife and house of my own, I still found myself at the time bent by the missed expectations of immigrant parents who had sacrificed almost everything for my education.

Another year had come to an end and I found myself onstage at the Marriott Cypress in Orlando yet again to accept another President's Club award for overachieving my sales goals.

I went on a right tear that evening to celebrate. Our Fortune 40 company had bought out Universal Studios for the night and an open bar was set up at every ride. I began seeing double as the padded shoulder harness grazed my belly and the Hulk Green Machine roller coaster whipped us around and upside down. The ride was aptly named; I turned a deep shade of emerald and my stomach revolted. Like a slingshot, the centrifugal force of the ride snapped the mouthful of vomit back onto my face and those of the riders around me. I don't quite remember how I got home or who cleaned me up, but I do remember a team of people pushing my fat ass up the stairs and onto the rented coach. I vaguely recall the walk of shame and the look of disgust of the riders as I shimmied to the back of the bus in my puke-stained clothes.

That behavior was only moderately worse than the year before, when I chose to celebrate the news of my President's Club trip to Ireland with a wobbly leap off the rope bridge at the Grand Cypress. I learned that night how nothing clears a Jacuzzi quicker than a bubbling dollop of vomit.

Many people left at the conclusion of the meeting, pursuing greener pastures only after the January bonus checks were cashed. A regional manager position became open and after lobbying the support of my current manager and obtaining a portfolio of customer reference letters, I applied for the job and flew up to Boston for my interview.

Our VP of sales was a stout, no-nonsense Irish American like myself. He was an inspiring, disciplined West Point grad who demanded a lot from his team and we were fiercely loyal to him. Though he was a few stations above me in the pecking order, I was never intimidated by him because he reminded me of my cousins and we enjoyed an easy, joking rapport.

"I was hoping you'd apply for this," he said with a sly smile, stroking the dimpled crease on his chin. "I've been waiting on this conversation for a long time."

He thumbed through the portfolio, nodding in approval as he turned each page.

"Everything looks in order!" he chirped.

"So, what's the next step?" I asked.

"Well, we're going to walk through why you're not moving forward. How's that for a start?"

He looked over his bifocals to make sure he caught the blood draining from my face. He cleared his throat and began.

"Here's what I see. I see a super-bright guy who is one of the most competitive people I know. You are an excellent sales rep and you can really turn that Irish charm on."

"Thanks," I stammered. "Sounds like there's a 'but' coming my way."

"All in due time," he said. "Here's another thing I see. You must be one of the funniest guys I know. For real. I almost pissed my pants laughing with you at the bar the other night and I have never seen someone hold court over a pint the way you do. I mean, everyone is just laughing around you. It really is amazing to watch you work the room!"

"Sounds like a guy people would want to follow if you ask me," I said in defense.

"Sure does. But here's another thing I see. This funny guy takes one look at the open bar at sales meetings and is magically transported back to a frat house. By the way, if you are wondering how you got into your room a few weeks ago, you can thank me for that.

"So, when I put two and two together, I have this funny guy who drinks a lot. Sounds like a drunk clown to me. Now, who wants to be led by a drunk clown? Do you?"

The color came back to my face immediately and I was flush with embarrassment; I mumbled a thank-you and started to back away from his desk.

"This wasn't an easy conversation for me to have either, Mike," he said. "I hope you do something with it and I do hope I can promote you when the time is right. That all depends on what you do with this gift I've just given you."

Some gift! Ultimately he hired this woman who didn't know anything about the laboratory distribution business over me! *Over me!* I outperformed for him and feathered the nest in which he sat his fat ass and this was the thanks I got!

"I can't believe he thinks that low of me!" I bellowed to my wife when I got home. "He had help thinking that way," was her dry response.

She was right, and being typically Irish, I was too thickheaded to notice. I never "inquired from within" to determine how I might have been cause in the matter. Perhaps I was the one who put all of those things in his head through my actions? He saw in me an enormous potential that was, like so many Irishmen before me, thwarted by the love of drink.

It was so easy to make him wrong and for about a week, I did. Once that was out of the way, I got driven.

I was obsessed with proving him wrong and raising his low opinion of me; I applied the same competitive spirit that had gotten me far in sales to this new task at hand. Backing away from the bottle was the easiest thing I had to do that year as I chowed down on the humble pie, rolled up my sleeves and offered to help the woman who got the job over me. I didn't care much for her and though I am not proud of it, I suppose at the time I applied my charm and got close to her in an effort to see what management saw in her that they didn't see in me. I took on extra tasks and spent hours working numbers with her as she tried to grasp the complexities of our business model.

This new manager would sputter in front of our eyes. She would call me sometimes at night in tears, sobbing how no one respected her and why the distribution culture might not be the right thing for her. Within 11 months she was gone and the search for a new manager began anew.

I flew up to Boston to meet the VP again, and dropped another portfolio on his desk. He stared at it for a moment and slid it over his blotter in my direction.

"I assume this is the same cock-and-bull story I read last year?"

"It is," I said, braced for another roundabout kick in the gut.

"But it's a very different person sitting in front of me now. You showed an incredible amount of grace in the face of difficult feedback and although I am sure you cursed me under your breath, you never let that show. That's a sign of class and that's also why you're getting the job this time."

Since then, I have led sales forces in a variety of roles, from line manager to senior director. Though I no longer work for that vice president, his name tops my list of references whenever I pursue a new position.

I have sometimes found myself in the unenviable position of rejecting a colleague's bid to move up the ladder and inspired by the leadership example of that man, I go to great lengths to provide constructive yet unvarnished feedback of what needs to be improved for the next career campaign.

Anyone who has ever worked for me has heard the drunk clown story at some point in our relationship because I am clear that if this drunk clown can make it this far by repairing a seemingly irreparable image, anyone can.

It's a good story and a valuable lesson in self-awareness, inquiring from within, and choosing to view a mentor's difficult feedback delivered straight with no chaser as the gift that it is.

Street Scholars

I took my father to a book signing at Paddy Reilly's the other day. For anyone not in the know, Paddy Reilly's Music Bar is a cultural gem that hosts live Irish music and literary events every night. Sadly, the bar is a rare and dying breed in Manhattan. Good luck trying to get a light beer on tap there; they are the only bar in the city that has nothing but Guinness on tap.

Paddy Reilly is a famous Irish balladeer but the bar is now run by Steve Duggan, an impish, tomato-faced man with manic eyes. He's pouring pints and always hustling. Despite a longstanding war with my newspaper and a "fuck the *Irish Voice*" banner on the wall, he has always appreciated my coverage of the music scene and the bands that play on his stage.

When I asked him if I could do a book signing in the bar once I wrote the masterpiece you are holding in your hands right now, he nodded enthusiastically. He handed me a card and encouraged me to call him when I had the thing written. I looked down at it and next to his name were the initials N.F.D.A.A.

"What does this stand for? Are you in some sort of trade organization?"

The blue eyes darted from side to side across his red face, scanning to see if any of the bar patrons were in for the setup.

"It stands for No Fucking Degree At All!"

With that, he banged a palm on the bar and convulsed with a case of the giggles.

"Did yeh like that?" he said in between fits of laughter.

Indeed I did, but I also marveled how forthright he was about his lack of education. He wore it like a badge, whereas my parents were ashamed of it.

"We never went to school but we met all the scholars on the way out," my Granny Cleary would say with not a small measure of pride. She'd point to the tight gray curls on her head.

"Yeh can't teach common sense in school and there are plenty of learned eejits walking around without it at those universities."

Granny Cleary left high school without finishing and went to work for a military family as a nanny. I'm sure the demanding general would strip the bed in disgust after Granny made it, rolling the linens in a ball on the floor and demanding the bed be made with sheets pulled tight enough to bounce a shilling. The ability to wrap things tight in sheets would come in handy in the small and primitive village of Ballylanders, where doctors were in short supply. She would be called on to dress sore wounds or to swaddle a newborn in a tight burrito of cloth. People knew she had no medical degree, but the skill of making the bed of a general, combined with an easy and caring mannerism, made her the go-to girl for patient care on this Tipperary outpost.

When you grow up with no electricity and few tools to work the farm, you become resourceful. My father is one to think of using the broom handle as leverage after his college-educated son throws his back out trying to lift something.

I am saving whatever I can to send my kids to higher education because I fear having N.F.D.A. on their business card is not going to get them far in this day and age.

But that's just me talking. If they decide to skip college altogether, it will be their choice. Lord knows they've met plenty of scholars without degrees on each branch of my family tree and that alone should prepare them for whatever life throws at them.

The Pharmacist with Limited Inventory

Would it shock you to learn I was a bartender once? Didn't think so.

You could say that being a bartender was in my genetic code but you would be wrong. My parents belonged to an ancient order called Pioneers, which required them to make a vow on their Confirmation day not to drink alcohol.

Genetics didn't get me behind the bar; financial ruin did. In college I never got the way that whole credit card thing worked; who knew there would be a $10,000 bill to pay at 19 percent interest after the last pint was bought on graduation day? I was forced to supplement my day job with a moonlighting gig to get myself out of debt and out of my parents' house within a year.

To make my folly worse, the only place that would give me a job after I graduated from the Woodbridge Bartending School in the Eighties was a newly opened Bennigan's.

Let me break this down for you. The now-defunct Bennigan's was to Irish people what Olive Garden is to Italians. It is a mass-marketed and processed attempt to re-create the convivial spirit of a cultural touchstone like an Irish pub or an Italian bistro.

What self-respecting Irish bartender would wear a kelly green polo shirt with rainbow suspenders? A barkeep in Ireland would get his arse kicked behind the stone wall of the pub if he showed up to work looking like that, and rightly so.

The manager's name was Frank, an Italian American with the kind of feathered hair that Chachi wore on *Happy Days*. Of course, he drove a

Camaro, clacked gum constantly in his perfect teeth, and left work early to sleep with any of the waitresses whenever he could.

"Yeah, I think this would be a good thing, having an Irish mick bastard like you behind the bar," he said, proud of his innate marketing genius as he contemplated launching the newest link on this chain of faux Irish pubs. "But first, I want to see you wait tables."

I pinned a giant "No, I'm not Tina Turner" button onto the rainbow suspenders and slung them over my shoulder, banking on the sight gag producing the good chemistry that brought the good tips. It worked and within weeks, I was promoted to the bar.

"I heard it said once that a bartender is a pharmacist with an extremely limited inventory," one of the older patrons said on my first day behind the green and wood-lacquered bar. He tossed his head in the direction of the parking lot. "You're gonna get all kinds of fucking crazies coming off Route 1. Be prepared for that!"

My favorite patron was a guy named Vince. He was a salesperson well into his fifties who managed to avoid the *Death of a Salesman* stigma you'd attach to most men still carrying a bag at his age. He was a slight man with white hair parted perfectly to the side. He had one brown eye that met your gaze intently and a glass eye that wandered wherever it pleased in his skull.

He would open the door and shout "Howdy, I'm here for the loose women and cheap beer" before saluting me on his way up the steps to the bar.

Once in a while, an enterprising hooker from the city of New Brunswick would come to our suburban bar to cast a line where the wealthier fish were. Sometimes they were easy to spot and Frank would unceremoniously launch them into the parking lot.

"We don't serve skanks here," he'd exclaim, smirking proudly. You could see the Camaro rock in the parking lot at the end of your shift and magically, the hooker would walk up to the bar a few days later looking for a drink.

The crowd was sparse one Sunday evening, with Vince on one end of the bar and the hooker on the other.

She shimmied over to him, waving away a wisp of hair that somehow escaped the onslaught of sprays and gels. She was pimpled but pretty, wearing a low-cut top with a ripped midriff that made her look like a Bon Jovi fan club reject. She was too smart to wear cliches like high-heeled boots and fishnets, but she also knew to show enough leg for marketing purposes.

"It sure is lonely around here," said Vince his good eye focused on the hooker. "How much is it gonna be, darling?"

Apparently, the thought of having sex with me was marginally more appealing than getting it on with a glass-eyed old pervert because she looked over at me like I was a wedge of lime sent to chase a shot of tequila.

"For both of you?" she pleaded, winking at me.

"Um, sure! Mikey, you're up for it, right?"

"I'm on duty, guys," I said, reaching for anything to polish.

"Let's take that as a yes, darlin'," Vince cooed. "You ever had grandpa sex?"

"No," she said tentatively, "but I think I'm gonna like it."

"You're gonna like grandpa sex," he said with a knowing smile. "That's when we do it all night until someone breaks a hip! Now, how much for a li'l, darlin'?"

"Five hundred dollars," came the reply.

Vince jerked his head so that both the good eye and the glass one met her gaze.

"That would be for the week, right?"

She threw her drink in his face and flounced out of the bar, never to be seen again. My bartending career ended once I had enough money to buy a shot of debt relief with a chaser of an apartment down payment, and I left the plastic paddy Irish bar in the dust.

Book 4: There Is No Revolution without Music
An Irish Voice for Music

Once upon a time, I read somewhere that good writing should inform, provoke, and/or entertain. Well, I hope at this point you have been entertained. I am quite sure some of my intensely private family members have been provoked by their perception that this book is "airing the family's dirty laundry," despite numerous assurances to the contrary by yours truly.

It has dawned on me that up until this point, I have done absolutely nothing to inform or educate. So, here goes.

Here's something I bet you didn't know. The Irish flag is green with a golden harp in the middle and it is the only national flag that has a musical instrument in it. That should tell you how important is to the soul and culture of the Irish people and I am mindful of that every week when I am putting together my "Off the Record" column for the *Irish Voice*.

If you subscribe to the notion that your writing career begins when someone actually pays you for it, then mine started the first day I wrote for the *Irish Voice*.

I'll never forget the day I first saw the advertisement in the classified ads seeking a music writer for "Off the Record." I had been a subscriber to the paper, one of the largest serving the Irish American community, for years. I had just gotten home from my job as a medical supply sales representative, flush with success over the $500,000 capital-equipment order that was in my briefcase. When I read that ad, I completely forgot about the order. At that moment, I realized that I needed more in a life that many would have considered to be already highly successful at that point; there was a lack of self-expression and a longing for creativity that was not being met within the design of my life. What follows are a few columns from the "Off the Record" page that somehow fit into all of this madness.

Sorry, Dad

The following essay appeared in the Irish Voice *to mark the 20th anniversary of the paper and my 10th as music columnist. Mom has it framed in her guest room, so I guess I did something right here.*

I'm not sure if that statement makes me great, but writing for the *Irish Voice* for more than a decade has drawn some blood. For that, I would like to apologize to one Mike Farragher of Tuam, County Galway, for the decade of abuse he never signed up for.

As he held his son at Margaret Hague Hospital in Jersey City 41 years ago, he clearly thought it would be nifty to name the new bundle of joy after himself. The Farragher name would live on, he would say, scrawling his signature on the birth certificate as he blinked back tears of pride.

Little did he know how that decision would bite him in the ass in 1997, when his bouncing baby boy started slinging ink for this fine weekly. Within weeks, the Irish and Irish Americans, who are not a shy bunch, would rough the new guy up in the editorial pages. The Southies would take me to task for being Bono's lapdog, the traddies would shred me for my blatant disregard for Irish cultural traditions, and the older set would say novenas for me as recompense for my blasphemous tones directed toward Saint Daniel O'Donnell.

My dad had retired that year to welcome his new granddaughter and tend to a peaceful garden of life in his golden years; however, nettles quickly rooted to choke his tranquility. "Our family name trashed in the letters pages," hissed one of my aunts. "Every week someone is calling Mike Farragher an eejit. This better not make it home to Galway."

It reached a boil about a month into my tenure, when I wrote "Byrne Bobby Byrne," a somewhat catty commentary on a certain hot bag of gas who blows show tunes and Irish parlor ditties through the pubs in my neck of the woods. Unbeknownst to me, it also served as a commentary of the blue-haired social scene in which my parents traveled (note the past tense). I happened upon my father, who that weekend paced around my kitchen like a caged leopard poked with a stick.

"That's my feckin' name on the article as well," he bellowed, punctuating my chest with his index finger for emphasis. "I won't be able to look Bobby Byrne in the face on his next boat cruise thanks to this, yeh eejit!"

"You think you're smart and funny," shrieked Mom in her Limerick accent. This is a devout, God-fearing, Sunday-school-teaching Catholic woman who loses all sense of charity when someone is down for the count. "I didn't carry you in my womb for nine months and educate you in the Catholic Church for you to form words like this. Such filth!"

So, this is an open apology to Dad. I am sorry that I dragged your good name in the mud. I signed up for the good, bad, and ugly when I took this job at the *Voice*; you did not. I hope you can find it in your heart to forgive me and if possible, reinstall my name in its proper place on your last will and testament. Above Brendan's. And if you can add a rider for that neat gold watch you wear on special occasions when Mom makes you wear a tie, it would be peachy! Bygones! Let this column serve as the Band-Aid to cover all the sores and scabs that your eldest son's quill has picked at over the years.

Writing this column means always having to leave the house with your insurance policy paid in full. There was that time when I paired the words "drug" and "addict" in a piece about Shane MacGowan when he played at Irving Plaza. Shocking, I know. He got so mad that I hid in a place he would never think to look—a dentist's office—until he staggered onto the tarmac en route to his Aer Lingus flight home. His entourage scowled at me during a reunion show last year, indicating that the word "forgiveness" is just a word between "fatal" and "f*ck off" in the dictionary to some people.

While "Off the Record" has put me off the Christmas Card list of Daniel O'Donnell, Margo, The Irish Tenors, The Celtic Tenors, Westlife, Boyzone, Louis Walsh, B*Witched, Frank Patterson (RIP), Shane MacGowan, Sinead O'Connor, Andy Cooney, Celtic Woman, Ronan Keating, Samantha

Mumba, Bobby Byrne, The Jersey Shore Women of Irish Heritage (who knew that so many of them were Bobby Byrne fans?), and countless parade committee chairmen across the country who have been crucified on these pages for offering lame entertainment at the summer Irish festivals, I have also been immensely blessed to count so many readers as friends.

I've stood by at close range while musical icons like Moya Brennan, Damien Dempsey, Joe Strummer, Boy George, Sinead O'Connor, Meg Griffin, Larry Kirwan, and many others would reveal the special sauce of their creative process during our chats. I've also tied lifelong bonds with publicists, radio disc jockeys, fellow writers, aspiring musicians, and many fans of Irish music who divined that an effervescent cultural cheerleader exists under this smartass persona if you bother to look.

I had a story I wanted to tell for many years that was blocked by my fear of what my parents and their neighbors might think. "You worry about what people think and your art dies," Sir Bob Geldof told me over coffee once as we discussed his last, deeply personal solo album. Armed with that, and six years of building a writing discipline entertaining (or provoking?) readers in these pages, I embarked on publishing *Collared*, a novel of sex abuse within the church. That was key to facing up to my own "complicated" relationship with a man of the cloth from my youth.

Apart from signing a much needed paycheck, Debbie McGoldrick and Niall O'Dowd of the Voice have been hugely supportive of my writing life, both inside and outside this newspaper. They backed that controversial novel without hesitation and were unequivocally rah-rah when I launched CelticLounge.com earlier this year.

They say you're not a writer until someone pays you for it, and their financial support meant much more than money. It was validation, and I thank them profusely for taking a chance on letting an unknown voice emerge within the pages of the *Irish Voice* all those years ago.

Writing "Off the Record" is also a valuable lesson to my children; they think I am famous because my picture is in the paper each week, and I use that artificial pedestal to lecture them on the benefits of reading and writing. Most tweens think flashing your junk during a Britney-style drunken dismount out of a limo is the only way to get your name in the paper, but my girls know better.

Most important, this column forged a new dimension in my relationship with my father. He's gotten callused over the years and is no longer bothered when he sees our name disparaged in the paper; we even laugh at some of the harsher critics who think I am the Antichrist with Microsoft Word. "They're gonna slaughter you next week," he says with a wink and a chuckle when a particularly hot column shimmers in the pages.

I was never the sports enthusiast that most dads look for in a son; my color commentary is reduced to statements like "the Cowboys are the ones in the silver tights, right?" It wouldn't leave us with much to talk about each weekend, and he would go off and talk sports with my brother in short order. That void of common ground during Sunday dinner ended 10 years ago with the question, "What are you writing about this week?"

New skin grows underneath scabs, and mine is thicker than ever. I am eternally grateful to the *Irish Voice* for all the growth—for myself, my father, and the constellation of artists I've been proud to help put on display.

An Open Letter to Festival
Organizers and Merchandisers

Hey Guys:

This summer sure flew by for me. I still can't believe I am putting away the double-wide white pants so quickly after taking them out of mothballs! Where the heck did August go, for chrissakes?

For you, I bet the summer can't move on quick enough. I can't remember a worse year for the Irish festival. Like the next Mel Gibson romantic comedy, you have yourself an attendance problem. Sure, you can blame the hot weather, the World Cup, the change in venue, and the economy. But the sad fact is that fewer people are buying what you're selling.

I just came in from the one in Wildwood, New Jersey, last weekend; the festival was run by a group of great people with the best intentions of promoting a culture. They had a great lineup of artists and a built-in crowd in this seaside summer vacation spot, yet they were scarcely able to attract only a couple of hundred people to their event.

The vendors were angrier than BP shareholders at an investor conference, meeting one another in the aisles to bemoan the lack of foot traffic. I'm not sure how well or poorly the event was promoted, but it is both Irish merchandisers and festival organizers alike responsible for this sad state of affairs.

You see 'em out dancing with their flat caps on/Wavin' their banners and tippin' their drum/And the blood runs deep/When the booze is cheap/Long as you ain't got an agenda to keep/You can be a Weekend Irish, hey!/Aye, aye, we're the Weekend Irish!

Those are lines I got from Kyf Brewer of Barleyjuice, from his song "Weekend Irish." It is a class of people to whom these vendors are clearly catering that leaves the rest of us feeling cold.

What's up with a certain sector of Irish Americans and their addiction to kelly green clownery? Do you ever see a real Irishman walking down Grafton Street wearing that loud crap? The drunks you see lining the curb on any given St. Patrick's Day parade, with their shamrock sunglasses, plastic green beer necklaces and emerald colored feather boas, look less like Irish people and more like the love child of Adam Lambert and the Jolly Green Giant. Ho, ho, no!

Look around any Irish shop here in America and you see the same fare. "Kiss me I'm Irish" buttons and green shirts made in China? Check. The flat caps with patchwork designs? Check. The aran sweaters that went out of style when the Clancys played Carnegie Hall in the Sixties? Check. The smattering of Guinness merchandise for the special alcoholic on your naughty list? Check, check, check! Is this what our culture is reduced to?

I have had a front-row seat on Irish culture during my time at the *Irish Voice* these last dozen or so years. I have been in the snug of a pub with Frank McCourt, sipped tea with Bob Geldof at Fitzpatrick's Hotel, and watched the nervous and bitten hands of Sinead O'Connor poke the air for emphasis during an interview. In all my time as a reporter, none of these artists ever came to the interview wearing a shamrock brooch or a plaid pair of pants. So where did this cartoonish depiction of the Irish come from?

I have a mind to gather all Irish merchandisers together on one school bus and drive them over to New Hope, Pennsylvania. It is there that the vibrant, innovative self-expression that I know in our artistic community is on full display at Celt-Iberia Traders. It is an eclectic and unique gallery and store inspired by the rich and culturally distinctive art and craft works of Ireland and Spain that are rarely, if ever, presented in the United States. The owners just moved to a bigger space, indicating that business is good.

It sounds weird mixing Irish and Spanish together, right? It's like serving soda bread with paella. Actually, there is a Galicia region in Spain that was populated by Irish and Scottish settlers. They blended with the local folk to create an offshoot of music and art that is every bit as Irish as a shamrock, but most Irish vendors are either too lazy or too scared to "mix Irish blood" to offer Galicia art to the summer Irish festival attendees. That is a shame.

In that shop that you'll be introduced to the works of Sharon McDaid, who works in textiles and mixed media in her studio on the Malin Road outside Carndonagh, on the way to Ireland's northernmost point, Malin Head. Her stuff is brilliant.

Sadly, Irish shops like the one I found in New Hope are few and far between. I applaud the likes of Mary Foley Reilly of the Irish Centre in Spring Lake, New Jersey. Sure, she stocks her store with some of the same green nonsense that everyone else does, but she also uses her showroom floor to promote the art of lesser known glass blowers, artisans, writers, and musicians whom Irish Americans might not know, in the hopes that a customer will slide a new cultural artifact into the bag along with their claddagh sweater. Fair play to her and we need more festival merchandisers thinking like that.

I actually tried to do something about this a few years back by joining one of the festival committees nearby. It was stocked with Shillelaghs and Hibernians a good deal older than me. They held their meetings in the back room of the bar, with most participants rolling dry tongues and licking their parched lips with one eye to the bar outside during the critical planning stages.

I remember broaching the subject of bringing Black 47 onto the roster but the universal consensus was that they were "too edgy." Now, there was certainly a time when the concept of mixing fiddles, political sentiment, and power chords was considered too dangerous in the early Nineties, which was when Larry Kirwan and the lads first came together. But the scene is now so crammed with bands that are in that genre, like Barleyjuice and The Prodigals, that the mixture of traditional and Irish music is virtually mainstream. Black 47, though still an immensely enjoyable rock act, is about as edgy as a butter knife 20 years later.

Instead, the organizers that year played it safe with a roster of folkies and the traddies that seem to share the same set list. "Fields of Athenry." "Irish Rover." "My Lagan Love." No, nay, never again, please!

The face of Ireland has changed forever and it is no longer an odd sight to see a Polish or African musician join a traditional seisún back on the auld sod. Even on this side of the Atlantic, artists like Susan McKeown are mixing it up with Yiddish musicians on her new *Saints and Tzadiks* album and tour, yet she was curiously absent from most festival lineups this year. With so many Irish people marrying Jews here in the States (as I have), one would think that a little out-of-the-box marketing to Jewish communities would bring more paying customers to our events.

And for the love of God, if I do decide to peel away to a remote outpost like East Durham for a weekend of Irish music, don't try to lock me into a mandatory four-day hotel package on a campground that I wouldn't park my (biological) mother-in-law's broom on! I'm all for making hay when the sun shines, but come on!

You may be thinking to yourself that the *Irish Voice* has some nerve bringing this up, especially after you advertised here in the paper. Understand my concern comes from self-preservation and I am not trying to bite the hand that feeds us. I derive my living as a culture vulture, commenting on the state of Irish and Irish American rock. If this scene goes away, so do I. I know after reading this you might think that would be a good thing, but we both know better.

Riverdance was successful at mixing Russian and gypsy styles into traditional music and dancing, which made being Irish hip again. The time is right for us to capture the imagination of a broader audience once more by embracing the changing face of Ireland instead of sticking to this warped ethos that appears to be trapped in a time when Maureen O'Hara was still of childbearing age and had real red hair.

What you're selling at Irish festivals might go down well to an older generation, but they are dying off at a shocking rate and the attendance records prove that.

To resume blockbuster attendance at these Irish festivals, I propose we put our heads together, maybe do some market research or online surveying, to get a sense of attitudes and the tolerance level for ticket prices. Any sales and marketing textbook tells you to find out what your audience needs and deliver it to them and online technology makes that much easier to do nowadays.

I'm not looking for a fight here, but I do think picking at a scab is the best way to heal the wounds of your balance sheet. If you need my help, drop me a line here at the office.

Still friends?
Mike

Mourning Music Stores

With the announcement last week that the Virgin megastores in Union Square and Times Square are closing, it's now easier to find an albino rat on the streets of Manhattan than it is finding a store that sells compact discs.

I know there are some of you out there reading the first paragraph and thinking that I am hanging onto these audio fossils known as compact discs; nothing could be further from the truth. With over 50,000 songs taking up 250 gigabytes on my portable hard drive, it is safe to assume that I have successfully made the transition to digital technology. That said, these store closures make me present to the fact that I can also be blamed for throwing a shovel of dirt on the record store, and for that, I am consumed with grief. This store is going out of business because I put it out of business, plain and simple.

The sense of impending loss has gotten so bad that I have visited a Virgin Megastore three times in the last week alone and have left each time with a bag full of CDs and hundreds of dollars charged to my debit card. T. Rex. Thin Lizzy. James Brown. Toots and the Maytals. ABBA (don't judge: guilty pleasure). Jaco Pastorious. The Black Eyed Peas. I am buying these relics at the fire sale price of $10 per CD as an act of penance for the digital sins that sit on my hard drive.

Of course, none of this makes sense. I will load these CDs into my disc drive and transfer the songs to my iPhone before putting the plastic relics on the shelf to collect dust. But as I prowl the aisles of the Virgin Megastore, I get swept up in the energy from the DJ booth and am stricken with a profound sadness for my own children. It is entirely feasible that they will have no memory of shopping in a music store.

Anyone of a certain age can remember purchasing that first album, your grooved licorice pizza wrapped in a colorful sleeve of cardboard adorned with genuine artwork. I was 13 in 1978 and I remember how adult I felt bringing my paper-route money to Harmony Hut in East Brunswick, New Jersey. I bought three things that afternoon that still form my musical vocabulary today: Kiss' *Alive II*, The Ramones' *Road to Ruin*, and The Rolling Stones' *Some Girls*.

Mike Marrone, now the program director of XM Radio's The Loft Channel, was the manager of the store when my 30-year music buying binge began, and I remember well the intense conversations we would have about Jackson Browne and The Police. The heavy metal was on my stereo and in my orthodontic braces and my descent into teenage hormonal hell began. I studied *Billboard* charts like a bookie and would go in an emotional tailspin when Peaches and Herb bested Elvis Costello in their positions. I have long given up actually getting assistance from the snot-nosed kids working at today's record store who were mere twinkles in their parents' eye when *Frampton Comes Alive* came out. But I miss the spontaneous critical debates that would break out in the aisles and the camaraderie sparked by a shared musical passion. I recently took up bass playing, which has led me to a new appreciation of funk, jazz, and reggae. A pretentious, portly jazz snob was hovering around the Miles Davis section at Virgin the last time I visited there and while his condescending tone was an annoying garnish, he did serve me with a meaty run through must-have jazz compilations that I would never get if I had to click my way through Amazon.com.

I am a huge fan of Steve Jobs and the portability of my music library; I feel completely naked if I walk out of the house without at least 15,000 songs on my iPod. Still, I also find myself missing the days when album artwork was as stimulating as the music inside of it. I bought Blondie's *Parallel Lines* because Deborah Harry was wearing nothing but a slip and a pair of Candies; I tucked that under the mattress because that and the JC Penney bra catalogue were the closest things to porn I could get my hormonal hands on at the time. It was a more innocent time back then, one that someone born in the digital age just won't understand.

New technology develops by the nanosecond and it usually yields progress, but I for one am not ready to let go of the record shop entirely. To many of us out there, music means a lot more than the drama of Chris Brown demonstrating his pimp hand to Rihanna or Britney Spears parading through nightclubs without undergarments. The music moves us and the album is a work of art to be judged as a whole and not as a $0.99 per click transaction. The more record stores close, the more we lose on that proposition.

Are you ready to give up on your local record store community? If not, let's make a pact that like a kid with a lemonade stand, we'll vow never to pass one by without buying something.

The Bass-ics

I had one of the most thrilling nights of my life recently: I played the U2 *Joshua Tree* album in its entirety. That doesn't sound out of the ordinary for an Irish rock columnist, you say? Well, here's the thing: I didn't just listen to that classic disc, I played along with it on my bass guitar.

I spent each Halloween smeared in grease paint in homage to Gene Simmons of Kiss, dreaming of one day playing the rhythmic sparks that emanated from his fire-breathing cartoon persona. I passed the last 12 years of my writing life here at the *Irish Voice* reporting about the music that I could never create myself. All that changed at the ripe age of 41, when I finally embarked on what had been a lifelong dream of playing a musical instrument.

"A few of us are going to jam tonight, wanna come?" asked my friend. He's recently divorced and decided to fill the emptiness of his house with rehearsal space—a ringing endorsement for all men to ditch their wives if ever there was one! I was always a spectator in these proceedings when he had "jam nights" in the past, providing wilted hand claps that may or may not have been in time with the beat if it was late in the evening or if I got hold of a few "bad pints" of Guinness at his bar. Did I mention the freedom of choice to install a new bar in the playroom is yet another endorsement for busting out of your matrimonial obligations? But I digress.

So there I was, in the middle of the mix, bringing the throbbing rhythm to the proceedings while two of my buddies flanked me at either side with guitars and percussion. It was a communion of the artistic and the sexual all at once, my hands stroking both the phallic neck and the hourglass, feminine-shaped bottom as Larry Mullen's sexy beats propelled the evening. I looked down, scarcely able to take in the sight of my fingers moving along the frets while my other hand plucked the right strings. My buds slapped my back and high-fived after each song and I contained a teardrop because it would be *so* un-rock 'n' roll to melt like a repentant celebrity on *The View* right about now. I was overwhelmed by the simple joy of keeping time and the thrill of spontaneous creation during an evening I will go to my grave remembering.

This whole thing started as an experiment in the power of positive thinking. Sound a little New Age-y? Perhaps. Sigmund Freud once remarked that the Irish are impervious to therapy and I tend to agree with him; at the same time, I can't resist the pop-culture mechanisms out there that boost your self-awareness and optimism, because they bring reality to your dreams. I sat through enough Landmark Education seminars and devoured enough books like *The Secret* to hear the same message loud and clear: if you speak it and put your mind to it, anything is possible.

So, it started with me speaking a little differently. The part of the Irish family tree facing the Limerick side is full of musical-bearing fruit; my mother, brother, uncle, aunt, and most cousins all know their way around a musical instrument. "Sure, the Galway crowd can't carry a tune on if it was lashed on their back," my father said to me one time as he shook his head and looked longingly at my mother making beautiful music on the fiddle. I shrugged, assuming that I took after dear old Dad; with the exception of a few high-stepping Irish dancers who compete professionally, it is a barren wasteland of any sort of artistic expression within my father's tribe.

Instead of telling people I am my father's son in all things music, I created the possibility through my promise that by the end of 2008, I would be able to play proficiently.

I have learned that while it is easy to speak this possibility, it is harder to actually play the bass guitar. I signed up for lessons and was greeted by Paul, my instructor. Walking into the place, I feel each of the many years that separate me from the instructors at the school; in fact, most of the people my age on the premises are dropping their kids off for their lessons. I am woefully conscious of how this raging midlife crisis might look to passersby as I spend time in the waiting room with my cherry-red bass while chums my children's ages pet their Mattel SpongeBob SquarePants guitars.

Word got out that I was going to "school to be cool," and my friends have been merciless in their teasing. "I love you and all, dude, but if you think I am gonna sit through a recital of 9-year-olds to hear you pull off 'With or Without You' on bass this June, you got another thing coming."

So here is where the power of positive thinking and possibilities met with reality as Paul shook my hand for the first time. We settled in, and I was fascinated with the shaking of his dreadlocks as his fingers moved effortlessly around the fret like supple blades of grass swayed by the breeze. His whole essence was riddim as he played a fluid line of reggae-fied funk. By contrast, my short and fat fingers chewed through the neck of the bass like sausages through a grinder. Trying to buzzsaw through the strings with alternating index and middle fingers as my other hand busied itself on the frets proved overwhelming. Whatever I was paying Paul to sit in the room and witness this could not be enough, I said to myself. Learning musical notes and keeping time seemed to be an insurmountable task in the beginning of the process. Most bass players flow effortlessly with the beat onstage, but try as I might, I couldn't wipe the constipated look off my face.

I often thought about throwing in the towel in the first few weeks, but there is no turning back now. I am obsessed! If you're looking for me at any given lunch hour, you can find me hunched over in the bass room at some Guitar Center or Sam Ash store. The shopping experience, however, is not always a pleasant one.

My tie grazes the strings and my ostentatious cufflinks clank along the frets as the underpaid staff, whose heavily tattooed arms and necks resemble partially completed coloring books, eye me with white-hot contempt. Of course, I am the white professional male embodiment of "The Man" who is cast as the villain who holds them back on the plot line in any one of their crappy unrecorded songs. Please allow me to introduce myself! I'm a man of wealth and taste; just call me Lucifer and I am turning up the volume and dedicating this version of "Under My Thumb" to all of you disenfranchised shoppers and clerks out there! If that act of defiance isn't punk with a capital "P," I don't know what is. It's only rock 'n' roll but I like it, beeyatches!

The cheap Dean bass I bought now has companionship; I have a tasty Hoffner violin bass knockoff in homage to Paul McCartney, and I am eyeing a vintage Fender American Jazz Bass whose purchase will likely be the tipping point between sending my kids to community college or university.

Our little jam session in my friend's basement is now a weekly appointment in my Blackberry, and in a few short weeks, we scaled and conquered the mountains of songs by the likes of Sublime, The Police, Neil Young, U2, and The Rolling Stones. With our advancing age and penchant for playing songs from the Eighties, we are thinking about calling ourselves "Old Wave" and playing for burgers on the local backyard barbecue circuit this summer. For an encore and a shot at an extra hot dog, I might even spit fire like Gene Simmons!

There are other life lessons learned that go beyond playing the bottom end of The Pretenders' "Mystery Achievement." Being a Leo, I am allergic to coaching of any sort. What a waste of time! I know everything! Slogging through finger exercises while the pre-pubescent virtuoso in the practice room next to yours plays Metallica bass lines will take anyone down a peg, which has been a healthy process. They say you can't teach old dogs new tricks, but I now know otherwise.

"F*ck this, it's too hard" is the catchphrase I grow fond of when I attempt to lose weight, find an agent for my novel, or do anything else that does not come to me as easily as I would like. At 41, the bass guitar has taught me that anything truly worth accomplishing takes perseverance. Scoff all you like, but I am living proof that if you say it, think it, dream it, and then do it, anything is possible.

Rock on!

Looking Back on a Musical Decade

I had been writing for the *Irish Voice* for a decade as 2009 came to a close, so I discussed with my editor the possibility of a comprehensive review of the millennium's best music from both sides of the Atlantic that included interviews with some of the artists who made the music. Selfishly, it would be a great way to sum up my 10 years as a music columnist for the paper.

Of course, technology changed the music business in the last 10 years as digital downloads killed record shops during this decade. I-Tunes picked up on our desire to buy music one song at a time instead of entire albums, putting the future of the album as an art form into question as we enter this next decade. So, this might be the last album decade retrospective of its kind. Who knows?

With that in mind, I came up with the following:

The best Irish rock albums of the decade

Afro Celt Sound System, *Volume 3: Further in Time*. The blueprint of this decade of global assimilation began with a band of Irish and African musicians who began to jam in Peter Gabriel's Real World Studios. Released on June 18, 2001, the Afro Celt Sound System's *Volume 3: Further in Time* was 70 minutes and 42 seconds of wicked international grooves that sound like nothing that came before or after it. Indian dhol drumming converges with furious uilleann pipe trills as Cork poet Iarla O'Lionaird calmly lays his gorgeous prose over this dance party. Peter Gabriel and Robert Plant do guest vocals in performances that are better than anything they've done on their own, but it is the brilliant chemistry of cultures that creates a new, thrilling take on Irish music.

Luka Bloom, *Innocence*. Christy Moore's kid brother gets lost in the music and begins a Middle Eastern chant in the middle of "Gypsy Music" as flute and bongo take the listener into a Moroccan rug market. Musically, *Innocence* is an international album, a possible reflection of a time in Irish history that saw the country playing host to immigrants hoping to roar with the Celtic Tiger "He stood and let the music glow, underneath his skin/He felt longing for Algeria, and loving for this song/How the music of a stranger helps the dreamer move along/The carpenter and the fiddler became the best of friends/And Mohamed lives in Galway, where the music never ends," he sings on "No Matter Where You Go, There You Are." There are many songs written about the Irish missing their homeland in a strange place. This might be the first one written from the perspective of someone missing home while living in Ireland.

The Saw Doctors, *The Cure*. These Tuam lads have always been the bog's answer to Bruce Springsteen. They spent the last 20 years spinning endearing stories with a reporter's eye for detail and a saxophone always at the ready. The band once again chronicled Irish life in their unique way. "The bones of our ancestors are buried in the field behind the shed/They could be lying there oblivious, underneath cement before I'm dead/Roundabouts and one-way streets/double yellow lines to beat the band/still takes you longer to get anywhere," sings Davy Carlton on "Out for a Smoke." "If Only" told of unexpressed love from the bog, while "Stars Over Cloughanover" was a starry-eyed view of the gorgeous skies overlooking Ireland's left coast. "Your Guitar" was a riff-heavy rocker and a loving look at domestic life about writing a song on the guitar that is a son's Christmas present. This album also told stories beyond the stone walls where the grass was green.

Sinead O'Connor, *Throw Down Your Arms*. Sinead flew to Kingston, gathering top Jamaican musicians including drummer Sly Dunbar, bassist Robbie Shakespeare, guitarist Mikey Chung and trombonist Nambo Robinson to record in Bob Marley's Tough Gong Studios. They lock into a ferocious roots groove from start to finish. The horns lock in with the rolling bass line and synth chopping on "Y Mas Gan," displaying a brilliant arrangement that was probably produced effortlessly. Much attention is paid to Marley when talking about reggae and roots music, for good reason, of course. Sinead shines a spotlight on Jamaican singer Burning Spear, giving the listener a new appreciation for an underappreciated talent. The rollicking bass line of "Marcus Garvey" and the slow-burning "Throw Down Your Arms" settles the world's problems in a mellow, dank cloud of ganja smoke.

VH1 Presents The Corrs Live in Dublin. On record, this band of hot Dundalk siblings sound a bit too scrubbed and polished for my liking. I have seen them in concert twice and both times, I was taken aback by their ferocity and muscularity. The folks at VH1 must have seen the same thing I did, and they rectified the situation by releasing a TV special and live CD in 2002. *VH1 Presents The Corrs Live in Dublin* saw the camera-ready clan show what they were made of on a small sound stage. The guitars on their monster hit "Breathless" chatter without the restraint of a fastidious producer, while the drums pound behind Andrea Corr's "breathless" cooing. She is a relentless flirt onstage, entertaining a number of high-wattage suitors throughout the evening. Bono strides onstage and engages in a heartfelt duet on Ryan Adams' "When the Stars Go Blue," turning their live version of that obscure song into a modest hit during the St. Patrick's Day season that year. He sticks around long enough to offer a cartoonish country western drawl on the Nancy Sinatra chestnut "Summer Wine." The disc also serves as a greatest-hits retrospective. Viewers unfamiliar with the band's back catalog got to hear the heavy Fleetwood Mac influence on tracks like "So Young" and "Radio."

U2, *All That You Can't Leave Behind*. My pick for album of the decade. "A mole, living in a hole/Digging up my soul/Going down, excavation/Love, lift me out of these blues/Won't you tell me something true/I believe in you," shouted Bono on U2's hit, "Elevation." It was if the line was written for New York in the wake of September 11, 2001. At least that's how it felt when I heard them playing it at Madison Square Garden a few weeks after the towers fell. "And if the night runs over/And if the day won't last/And if your way should falter/Along the stony pass/It's just a moment, this time will pass," Bono sang on "Stuck in a Moment That You Can't Get Out Of." Was Bono some rock 'n' roll Nostradamus, predicting this moment of public mourning when he wrote those lines in Dublin a year before America's most famous tragedy? "All That You Can't Leave Behind" might be packed with uplifting radio-friendly classics, but to myself and many New Yorkers I know, this album pulled us through our darkest days.

The Best Irish American albums of the decade

The best Irish American music of the decade rivals the Irish albums in spirit, creativity, and love of Irish culture. You may be inspired to go on LimeWire or one of the many free sites to download these albums. Please don't. Go on i-Tunes and buy them or visit the bands' websites and buy the songs directly from them. If you can find an actual CD store still open, fair play to yeh! Go there above all else.

All of these artists work tirelessly on the road and are our best hope at keeping Irish culture alive in an era of digital downloads and declining pub attendance. Make a New Year's resolution or some other promise to yourself to see every one of these bands in the next 12 months. It will show bar owners here in the States that Irish rock can still pack 'em in!

The Prodigals, *Needs Must When the Devil Drives.* "I do have certain, very specific feelings connected with that album," says Prodigals leader Gregory Grene when asked to reflect on *Needs Must,* the band's album from 2003. "This album was recorded immediately following two seminal events in my life—one was the passing of my father, and the other was the birth of my daughter." There was also another set of lineup changes in store for the band that bled into the recording process. Singer Colm O'Brien added a hoarse and gritty barroom feel to the tidy soda bread soul of the band—if Grene was the jig, O'Brien was the punk in this jig punk outfit at the time. "We just found out that Colm was going to be leaving the band, to have his own lovely kid, and that lent a poignant resonance to the recording as well," Grene said. He didn't leave before contributing to some Prodigals classics, including "Uncle Arthur," a drunken sing-along to founder of the famous Guinness brewery, and "Ball of Alcohol," a ferocious rave-up in which he screams, "I can't get drunk enough."

Enter the Haggis, *Casualties of Retail.* From the metallic stomp of "Music Box" to the Appalachian hayseed sound of "Another Round," this Canadian Scotch-Irish outfit touches on a dizzying array of textures to achieve a modern Celtic classic on this disc. Fiddles howl like lost souls moaning for a spare prayer, while the band's pristine harmonies, especially on the prog-rock instrumentals "Congress" and "Martha Stuart," come shining through. They slow things down briefly for an introspective "She Moved Through the Fair," giving the listener a much-needed break from the ferocity. "We were definitely pretty proud of what we'd done at the time and were excited to get it to the fans," singer Trevor Lewington says. "That being said, after listening to the same songs every day for a month straight, you're happy for some time away from the music. Shortly after the album was released it was clearly a fan favorite, and tracks such as 'Gasoline,' 'Down With the Ship' and 'Congress' stood out as hits for the band." Enter the Haggis also gives back to the Celtic community by putting out Rootstomp compilations, which offer a showcase to lesser known Celtic bands. Check them out on enterthehaggis.com.

Dropkick Murphys, *Blackout*. Like most Irish punk outfits, Dropkick Murphys toiled away for years in the shadow of The Pogues. By the time they released *Blackout* in 2003, they had fashioned those influences into one loud, raucous, chaotic mix that stood in its own genre. "So you say you fell in love and you're gonna get married/raise yourself a family, how simple life can be/somewhere it all went wrong and your plans just fell apart/and you ain't got the heart to finish what you started," screams lead singer Al Barr on the album's opener, "Walk Away." The track sparks with shooting guitars and thundering drums as Barr lends an angry voice to "the ones that you loved and left behind." Dropkick Murphys honor the ancient art of storytelling with some wicked covers of traditional classics. "Fields of Athenry" plays up the Irish defiance in the face of starvation and famine, while "Black Velvet Band" is a hopped-up jig of molten lava. If this band is not in the jukebox of your Irish bar, you are well advised to find another Irish bar! To hear samples of *Blackout*, check out dropkickmurphys.com.

Pierce Turner, *3 Minute World*. This is an orchestral pop masterpiece, plain and simple. We may all argue over what albums deserve to be on a list like this, but no one will argue that Turner is one of the most original voices on this list or any other, for that matter. A record obsessed with time, Turner vacillates with measuring it and reflecting on how it slips through the fingers like sand. Time is everywhere—the ticking of clock parts provides percussion and their chimes are cymbal crashes. A dreamy merry-go-round melody induces drowsiness on "You Won't Mind" as Turner lazily mourns the fact that he has missed his train. "I'm a busy man/I'm up to my eyes but I remain calm/have you seen the time/honest to goodness how the days fly by/I have to find a pair of socks I could live with plus a T-shirt that's cleaner than the one I wore to bed," he sings on "Busy Man" as whimsical strings and chimes float in the background. It's surreal and cinematic stuff, like a musical concoction made by Charlie and the Chocolate Factory. Check him out at pierceturner.com.

Black 47, *Trouble in the Land.* My vote for Irish American album of the decade, substantiated by the results of the reader's poll we conducted online around this list. This band became the musical soundtrack of Irish America in the Nineties. With a recent wave of Irish immigrants flooding into New York during the late Eighties, a hunger for home drove a new musical genre in the bars of Bainbridge Avenue.

On a personal level, their music awakened in me a love of Irish music. After suffering through decades in a house where I had no control of the stereo, I rebelled against all forms of Irish music my parents played. When I first heard the mixture of traditional Irish melodies, reggae, rock, and punk played with such wanton disregard for the sacredness of our culture, I was hooked on Black 47 and Irish music from that moment on. It's not a stretch to say that if it weren't for my exposure to Black 47, I would not have become so engaged in my Irish roots and would not have had any business writing a column on Irish music, and there would have been no writing life and no book about the effect of shamrocks on your brain! Black 47 rose to stardom by combining Irish melodies with gritty hip-hop beats, caustic raps about British rule and driving riffs swept off the floor at CBGBs. By 2000, the band had seen fame come and go. Their 15 minutes of MTV fame had come and gone, founding member Chris Byrne was about to depart, and lead singer Larry Kirwan was running out of gas. The band used that angst to create the gritty *Trouble in the Land* in 2000. As was the band's trademark, they touched on a dizzying array of musical influences. "Those Saints" was a Mardi Gras parade, "Desperate" was a swaying reggae cocktail, and "I Got Laid on James Joyce's Grave" was an injection of snarling punk energy. Their Irishness is front and center on "Bodhráns on the Brain," a hilarious rocker about Kirwan's beat-crazy girlfriend who gets wooed by a Bodhrán maker. "More power to your elbow!" the girlfriend shouts when Kirwan can't keep up the pace. "We were experimenting melding jazz, gospel, funk and other genres with revved up Irish rock-trad," says Kirwan. "There was a general what-the-hell feeling of stretching out, seeing what would happen before the bloody boulder dropped. The high for me was melding the hip-hop, New Orleans jazz, and Irish trad influences in 'Those Saints,' and capturing the biographical ache of the two ballads, 'Falling Off the Edge of America,' and 'Tramps Heartbreak.'" *Trouble in the Land* sounds like a greatest hits Black 47 album, encapsulating everything that makes them great. Check them out on Black47.com.

Vintage Vinyl

So I thought I'd finish this book out strong by riding the car through Memory Lane to see if I could come up with a pearl of wisdom or a lightning bolt of literary genius before my deadline. I mean, any one of the five autobiographies from Mark Twain that are planned for imminent release may very well be competing for time with these essays on your Kindle, so I am feeling the heat!

Memory Lane for me is a state road clogged with congestion and retail plaque known as the U.S. 1 corridor in Middlesex County, New Jersey. The epicenter of said memory lane is in a neighborhood between the outskirts of the rusted industrial landscape that one would see in their initial descent to Newark Airport and just out of reach of the saltwater taffy promise that is the Jersey shoreline.

I pulled into the parking lot of Vintage Vinyl Records in Fords. I have pumped hundreds of dollars of paper route and babysitting money into this place over the years and if there were any memories worth sharing, they would be in here! It was recently voted one of the best record stores in the country by *Rolling Stone*, and Ozzy Osbourne even did a record signing here not long ago, though you wouldn't know it from looking at the place.

Potholes in the parking lot jostled me inside the creature comforts of the Caddy as tumbleweeds of discarded fast food takeout bags blew a path in front of me. A once popular nightclub in this strip mall had been converted into a hookah bar in deference to the Indian American community that has commandeered the local real estate. Discarded bits of paper clung to the chain link fence on the perimeter of the parking lot, adding to the hint of desolation.

One step into Vintage Vinyl and I knew I was home.

Record stores have that smell like no other; a mixture that hints at the rolling of a wet dog's ass in dried cardboard. Some grating aggressive metal thunders out of the speakers above, expressing the collective rage of each discarded compact disc in the bargain bins that have been left behind by technology.

There was a time when Vintage Vinyl stocked all the latest vinyl albums and compact discs that were on the charts. The real gold could be found in their import section, where they would have the only copy of the Siouxsie and the Banshees/Robert Smith collaboration in the Garden State. Today, the store makes a living buying CDs from laid-off workers or cash-starved college students. That merchandise started with a list price of $15 and is now bought for $2 before a new $4 retail price is set in the used CD section. Before you make the store wrong for these predatory practices, keep in mind that each time we downloaded a track from our desktop on i-Tunes, we made this store die a little more.

Tattooed bikers shuffle intently through the hard rock section, eyeing me suspiciously. A heavily pierced punk rocker in skinny jeans shoots a look dripping in judgment as he alphabetizes the jewel cases. With an electric-blue streak running through his spiked black hair and an arm so tatted it looks like an unfinished coloring book has been wrapped around it, you wonder, *who the hell else but Vintage Vinyl would employ this jerkoff?*

It was then that I noticed that I was the only patron not sporting an earring or a black T-shirt; the tie draped over my well-fed gut and the receding hairline made me look like every white-collared boss that held their economic advancement under his thumb. They don't see the punk-rock heart bleeding a funky black inside my chest; they just see a cat amongst the pigeons.

I plucked an out-of-print used copy of Culture Club's *Kissing to Be Clever*, sandwiched it between two vintage ska discs to avoid detection and embarrassment, and made my way to the checkout counter. Bon Jovi, a local musician of this county, would get his ass kicked by these hardcore Slayer fans for darkening the door of this place and branding New Jersey as the home of light mousse metal.

Rightly so.

He recently had a hit with the song "Who Says You Can't Go Home?" and for the crime of lying to me, I am inclined to kick his ass as well.

Well, what do you think? Was that an ending worthy of Mark Twain?

I probably shouldn't have ended this on such an angry note. Twain himself said, "Anger is an acid that can do more harm to the vessel in which it is stored than anything on which it is poured."

I'll drink to that.